Prepared for publication

By
HISTORIC PULISHING

Life and Labors of Rev. Jordan W. Early,
One of the Pioneers of African Methodism in the West and South

Sarah J. W. Early

Jordan W. Early

LIFE AND LABORS
OF
REV. JORDAN W. EARLY,
One of the Pioneers of African Methodism in the West and South.

BY

SARAH J. W. EARLY.

"Cœlitus mihi vires."

NASHVILLE, TENN.:
PUBLISHING HOUSE A. M. E. CHURCH SUNDAY SCHOOL
UNION.
1894.

CONTENTS.

PREFACE.

To put on record some of the principal events which transpired during the life and labors of the early pioneers of African Methodism, seems to be a duty we owe to those worthy men who have preceded us in the arduous work of establishing a Church attended with such wonderful advantages to the colored people of this country. Blind must the man be who cannot see the design of Providence in prompting the hearts of men to resent the religious intolerance which was hurled against them just at the time when the increasing weight of the yoke of bondage bore so heavily on an already oppressed race that they felt its weight could be carried no further, and that they should build for themselves an institution which should be a harbinger of the great freedom which was so soon to follow. This institution, whose foundation was laid with such wonderful care and labor, has done more to convince the world that colored men possessed in a high degree the power of self-government, and that their hearts swelled with the same love of liberty which animated the hearts of the most noble of earth's sons. The phenomenal success of the Church which had its origin in adversity and obscurity, the offspring's of the minds of men whom the world consider uncultured and inexperienced, its rapid development and advancement, its power to surmount all obstacles and its final and signal success, awakens the admiration and wonder of the Christian world. We do not wonder that those who now live and enjoy the great advantages afforded by this strong and prosperous body, should desire to know something of the character and labors of those men who were the favored instruments in the hands of God, by which he established an institution that has done more to develop the moral force and executive power of the descendants of Africa in America than has been accomplished by any other means. It is certain that we have on record no class of men since the days of the Apostles, who having had no intellectual advantages or moral training, who have accomplished such notable work in the enlightenment and elevation and Christianizing a people who were doomed to ignorance, servitude and degradation as have done that class of men. No one can witness the effect of their ready foresight, their wise counsel and heroic actions under such trying circumstances, without being filled with wonder at the amazing goodness of God in directing their course, and admiration for the power that led them with unerring precision through the dark mazes of superstition and oppression, to such signal victory. They trusted in God with faith scarcely less fervent than that of the primitive Christians. They were men of eminent piety and sound integrity, and there was a silent energy accompanying their labors, though done in an unostentatious manner that gave them success wherever engaged and silenced all opposition. Thus the subject of our narrative was one of the favored ones who were permitted to take an active part in establishing and building up the A. M. E. Church in the Western and Southern states.

It is not possible to find all the data accompanying the labors of those men who laid the foundation of the Church. There were but few writers among them, and those who could were too modest to record what they thought to be simply their duty. Not expecting nor wishing for notoriety in this life, they labored in faith, looking only for the reward which was promised in the life to come. Of much of the most important labors of J. W. Early, the date cannot be accurately ascertained; but the facts are still fresh in his memory, and authenticated by many witnesses.

Life and Labors of Rev. Jordan W. Early.

CHAPTER I.

It has often been said of men who have made themselves notable in the world by accomplishing great and noble deeds, or, by their peculiar intellectual ability that their notoriety was the consequence of their superior training in their youthful days. It is also alleged of those men who have done the most to elevate mankind religiously, and to refine them morally, are those who received their moral and religious training from a good and pious mother, or inherited their virtues from a father of exalted principles; that their intellects developed and their virtues matured in accordance to the prayers of Christian parents and the environment of comforts and seclusion from vice. But this was not the case with the subject of this narrative. Though humble and destitute in early life, God, who presides over the destinies of all men, raised him up to be a blessing to the generation in which he lived.

Jordan Winston Early, was born in Franklin County, Virginia, on the 17th day of June, in the year of our Lord 1814, and there spent the days of his early childhood enjoying life as best he could, according to surrounding circumstances. At the age of three years he and two younger brothers were left orphans by the death of their mother. "Though so young," he says, in after years, "no one can realize the desolation and loneliness which I suffered after I had seen my mother borne to the grave, for myself and all my relatives were in a state of bondage and I had no one on which to depend for care and protection. But God who hears the young ravens when they cry had compassion upon us and kept us from want and from surrounding evils." He says, "I had an affectionate aunt who would gladly have administered to our wants, and did give to us all the time she could spare, but that was very little, being herself a slave and consequently absent most of her time. There was an old lady called "Aunt Milly," in whose care the children of the plantation were placed while their mothers labored in the field or elsewhere, to whose care I and my brothers were consigned. She was a devout Christian and was rich in faith toward God and in good works. With unfaltering confidence in God she prayed for the children that He would lead them in the right way. Her belief in God's word was strong, and she relied daily on His promises that He would eventually fulfill her most ardent desire. Often have I seen her rise from her scanty bed at the hour of midnight and beseech her Heavenly Father with tears for the salvation and future well-being of the children placed in her charge. God's ear was certainly attentive to the cry of his humble disciple, for all those children began early to develop the better qualities of their nature and, in despite of their unhappy surroundings, became useful and intelligent men and women. Blessed foster mother! Surely, if her glorified spirit were permitted to see earth's sorrowing children struggling to overcome the difficulties that assail them in their upward journey, she beckons them onward and points them to the crown which is laid up for the faithful at God's right hand It is scarcely necessary to say that a child living according to the surroundings of slavery, and an orphan also, would have many sad and lonely hours and be seriously impressed with the inequalities of life by being near those children who were the subjects of parental care and enjoying the advantages of education and social refinement. "I could not then comprehend why my Heavenly Father should deprive one of all earthly advantages and enjoyments and lavish them so profusely upon another."

Young Early gave remarkable attention to the counsel of older and more experienced persons than himself and always showed an intense desire to conform his life to the best rules of integrity, and that his conduct should be as near as possible without reproach. He was lively and playful at times, but was mostly serious and meditative. He was brave and industrious and always strove to acquire some means which he could call his own. He entertained a great love for the sight of natural objects, especially the scenes of night, and would often stand for hours and gaze at the sparkling beauty of the starry heavens, and in awe and wonder listen to the accounts given of their amazing magnitude and of their wonderful distances from us and each other. He says, "I had an uncle who was very intelligent. He had been a sailor and had visited many lands and had acquired much useful knowledge of many things both on land and sea. He had great regard for the sciences, but he loved astronomy, of which he had picked up considerable knowledge, best of all. My uncle loved to go and hunt at night. I always accompanied him when possible, and never wearied of hearing him tell about the motions and other properties of the stars, and of the relations they bear to each other." His mind was led by this means to contemplate the majesty and goodness of God, as seen through his visible works, and was carried from the unhappy surroundings with which it was environed, that of slavery and degradation, to something higher and holier and more ennobling. "I felt" says he "whenever I looked on any of the mighty works of God a sensation stealing over me of a kindred intelligence calling me to mount upward and enjoy a better existence which awaited me beyond the present."

Early was always religiously inclined. He says, "I loved the sound of sacred song and what little I could hear of the word of God. I often pondered over it in silence, and strove to comprehend its meaning." He early learned the Lord's Prayer and loved to repeat it with reverence and gratitude. As there were no schools for colored children in those days and no books given them to read, the best that they could do was to learn snatches of songs and passages of Scripture which they gathered from quotations recited in the imperfect sermons which they heard. But oh! how they thirsted for knowledge, that inestimable boon which exalts humanity to a nobler manhood. They could not comprehend why it was lavished so bountifully on others, but denied to them. But they determined to use all the means that they could command for this purpose. Though almost destitute of clothing and no shoes, he and others would run many miles to camp meetings and religious associations, and when there would climb convenient trees and thus find seats out of the way of men and women so that they might see what transpired and hear what was said, and thus the performances of the ordinances of the Church were stamped indelibly on their minds. God was furnishing the means for their enlightenment, which afforded them the skill to conduct their own Church affairs when grown to manhood and maturity.

CHAPTER II.

About the year 1826 the Early family removed from the State of Virginia to that of Missouri. "I was delighted," he says "with the prospects of new scenes and new acquaintances. I was strong, healthy and active, and traveled most of the way, which was about eleven hundred miles, on foot, and in this way had an opportunity to see much of the intervening country, and to occasionally engage in the chase of which I was very fond.

"Having arrived in my adopted state, I repaired to the city of St. Louis, where I soon found companions suitable to my age and tastes. We had our lively sports and happy hours of greeting, but we did not forget or neglect the Church." He with his companions, of which he was a leader, often visited the churches of the various denominations to listen to and comment on the sermons and other exercises. These were among the severest days of oppression, but the colored people were sometimes allowed to have sermons preached to them by white ministers. "One Sabbath evening my companions and I went to hear one Mr. Barger who was notable for his piety and good works. He preached a wonderfully impressive sermon to young people, telling them of their often repeated promises to begin a better life and leave off their sins by repentance toward God; but they had as often violated those promises and deferred the acceptance of a free salvation, thus slighting the offers of a compassionate Saviour. While listening to his discourse, I felt that every word was aimed at me, the truth of which struck my heart as a hammer, and went through my bones like fire. I sank down under a sense of the awful weight of guilt that rested upon me. My companions left me and fled; but I could only call upon God to extend his mercy to me, a poor sinner. My conviction was deep and powerful, and I continued to pray. After remaining in prayer and supplication for three or four days I was enabled to exercise faith in the merits of my blessed Redeemer. The burden of my sins rolled away and my heart was set at liberty. I was exultant in the love of God, and my mouth was filled with praises to the Lamb who had redeemed me and washed me in his own blood, and made me an heir with himself and a priest to God. As I stood amazed with this wonderful development of God's goodness to me, I took a retrospect of my past life. I could see myself following my mother to the grave while almost an infant, riding on my little stick horse curbed with a bark bridle, the only cortege I could afford then. I saw myself looking into the open grave, ready to receive all that was dear to me and my only support and protection. Too young to comprehend the awful meaning of the occasion, I turned away to go to my little pallet in our desolate cabin to call in vain for mother and weep myself to sleep. From thence God's goodness had followed me every step of my pathway until the present, and now had filled me unutterably full of his love. I exclaimed, It is an answer to the prayers of my good old foster mother. I immediately consecrated my life to his service, which I felt would be too short to perfect his praise. This was in the year 1828. I united with the church without delay and was baptized around the holy altar of the same church in which I was convicted." Early had a good voice for singing, an exercise in which he was almost always engaged. His voice could always be heard in the mellow strains of the church music in which he delighted to join. This was a power which he employed for doing much good in after years.

Immediately after joining the church, Early says he felt a strong impulse to do something definite in the Master's cause. He was allowed to lead prayer meetings and to lead singing, and to assist in other duties of the church. He was appointed Superintendent of the Sunday-school, in which he obtained good success. He took much delight in performing such duties as he was able, and in them he felt great liberty. But this work did not satisfy the longings of his soul. He had heard a voice within calling him to a higher and nobler work than man could prescribe for him. He was not disobedient to the heavenly injunction, but commenced at once to exhort his fellowmen to flee from the wrath to come, and wherever he could find the opportunity he did not fail to proclaim the message received from God for the redemption of his fellowman.

In the year 1833, Early received an exhorter's license from the M. E. Church, and continued in the good work. "In the meanwhile," says he, "I embraced every opportunity to improve my mind so that I might be better prepared to perform the duties that were incumbent upon me in my religious career. When about eighteen years of age I formed a resolution that I would learn to read and write. Being in bondage, of course, I had no opportunity to attend school. I made my desires known to a Presbyterian minister who seemed to have great sympathy for me. He proposed to teach me in the evenings if I would come to him. I gladly accepted the offer and began at once to receive lessons. My progress was slow, for I had often to be absent from the city on my trips up and down the river; but I persevered until I could read well enough to serve all my purposes. While the boat on which I was employed was plying between New Orleans and St. Louis, the mate was kind enough to give me writing lessons. In those days we had no printed copies; so he proposed to write them for me and I was extremely glad of the offered favors. Though these opportunities were meager and cost me money, they were gratefully accepted as being of invaluable service to me. Thus I applied myself to the task and employed all the spare moments I could command, until I could write a creditable hand. In this way the good Lord provided for the future in putting it into my heart to learn what I could, so that I might be one of the pioneers of African Methodism in the Western States." He further says:

"If I could then have seen the many thousands before whom I would stand in the future, I would have exclaimed, Lord I am too small for the great work required of me. But then I found this precious promise to be true: 'Sufficient unto the day shall thy strength be.' Step by step was I led by his Spirit, and hour by hour was I protected by his mercy, till my whole being, my time, my talent, and all I had, was absorbed in his work."

CHAPTER III.

Up to this time, 1832, Early had been a member of the Methodist Episcopal Church, but now African Methodism had been introduced and a small membership had organized themselves into a church, with the efforts of Rev. William Paul Quinn. In so doing he saw that his usefulness would be greatly extended, and that he could have better access to his people. "I had been some years preparing myself for the Gospel," he says, "and I had acquired some experience in the work. In the year 1836 I applied for a license to preach, and received it from the hand of Rev. George W. Johnson who had come to us from the Ohio Conference.

"William Paul Quinn, the indomitable leader of African Methodism in the West, as I have already stated, had introduced it in the city of St. Louis, and Brooklyn, Illinois, but the people of that persuasion had no houses in which to worship. Thus far their meetings were all held in private houses, and on account of the growing power of slavery they were necessarily obliged to proceed very cautiously, but they often consulted about the utility of making preparations to permanently establish and build up the Church. For they were persuaded that it would be the Church of all others peculiarly adapted to their present want. The spirit of independence demonstrated by their retiring to themselves to avoid the humiliating circumstances in which proscription placed them, and that they might independently transact their own business, thrilled the hearts of many intelligent persons with joy."

Early and some others obtained a small log cabin near the end of Main street in which they began to hold meetings. They earnestly solicited the attendance of their many friends. Great was their rejoicing when they could meet "under their own vine and fig tree," and the members increased rapidly. So much did they grow in favor with the people that after awhile they found it necessary to seek for better quarters, for which purpose they empowered a committee to negotiate. They obtained an old mission house from the Presbyterians, on the corner of Seventh and Washington streets. "This," says he, "we repaired and made stronger, and decorated so as to be quite comfortable and attractive." The public gladly tendered their help and sympathy, and they had frequent outpourings of the Holy Spirit which greatly encouraged them to press forward in their good work. Though they could not see to the end, their faith was strong and they felt that they were moved by a supernatural power and led by an unseen hand, which was soon to bring them out of the house of bondage and wilderness of superstition into the fair land of freedom and prosperity. To worship God without fear or molestation was a boon for which they scarcely dared to ask. To have the privilege of obtaining moral or religious training, free of those terrible restrictions to which prejudice and power subjected them, was something for which they had not dared to hope. But still they struggled on. God was preparing them for a bright and noble future.

In the year 1832 was about the time of Nat Turner's insurrection, on account of which the colored people suffered untold barbarity and persecution in many of the Southern states. These were perilous times, and none but men and women of the bravest hearts and most daring minds were able to brook the terrible pressure of the law and public sentiment. This faithful band was forbidden to hold night meetings unless preached to by a white man, while others were prevented from attending at all. Early was very closely allied to a certain friend named Martial. These two young men had made themselves very useful among the better class of rich people, and had in this way obtained much favor and respect from them. These readily recommended them to the authorities of the city and solicited their favor in behalf of their cause in church matters. The Mayor and others prevented the patrol, who were ever present, from injuring or arresting them and otherwise maltreating them, so their meetings in the mission house were gloriously successful, and notwithstanding all these obstacles, grew in interest continually. Early says, "In the meantime I exhorted and preached, having charge of the church when there was no regular preacher present, and assisting as steward and trustee, when we could obtain the services of any one for a time, and in conducting the financial interests of the church and building up the Sabbath-school. Scores of souls were converted to God and added to the church under the labors of the faithful servants of God when they could be obtained, and the never-ceasing vigilance of these young men who labored in the cause of Christ because they loved it, and propagated the cause of African Methodism, because it partially satiated their thirst for freedom and progress, which began to stir the hearts of all intelligent colored people. The mission house now began to be too small to accommodate the large and intelligent audiences that attended their meetings, so they obtained a large hall on Broadway, over the engine house, near the centre of the city, and held their meetings there. As our members still increased and our meetings became more popular, we began to discuss the propriety of buying a lot and building a suitable edifice in which to worship God." Through years of struggle and toil they had pursued with undeviating purpose the object of their intense desire, and now they can see the accomplishment just ahead of all their ardent wishes.

If we notice these years of progress, we can perceive how human efforts develop ability, and what effect freedom of speech and united action have in enlightening and elevating true manhood. Weak and helpless in the humility of their beginning, they have expanded in magnitude and grown in power, until their influence is felt in every department of society. They commenced as soon as circumstances would permit, to devise means to get money and lay it by until they could gather a sufficient quantity to make the purchase of a lot. At the end of two years they found a lot on the corner of Eleventh and Green streets for sale. They bought it and commenced to build. Says Early, "I entered fully into the work, giving my money, my time, and all the talent that I had, for what I deemed to be such a glorious work. All hands assisted with might and will. The women, as well as the men, did most valiant work, both in giving and collecting money, and in due time the Church arose to the exceeding joy and satisfaction of all concerned. The church was built of brick. It had an audience room and gallery, and was seated with pews. There was also a basement where the Sabbath-school and classes were to meet. It cost five thousand dollars, which was a great sum for those days." They felt strong in taking possession of their new house. They were now a fully organized and progressive church, with their trustees, stewards, leaders, and salaried pastor.

Early says, "None rejoiced with more solid joy than I did, for I had labored so long and hard to accomplish this object, and now it was completed and stood as a monument of the mercies of God." This was in the year 1840.

CHAPTER IV.

Previous to 1840. Early had been ordained to deacon's orders at the Annual Conference which met at Indianapolis, Ind., in the year 1838. This fact gave him a better opportunity to labor for the Church, and to further expand the capacity he had already acquired. He had often felt a desire to extend the work wherever opportunities would permit, and he says, "I let none pass me which I did not improve. I had occasion to remain some time in the cities of Burlington and Dubuque, Iowa. While there I engaged heartily in the Church work, and I trust that I was the humble instrument in bringing souls to Christ. From thence I passed on to Galena, Ill., where my business often called me. While there the thought occurred to me to establish an A. M. E. Church in that place. I called the people together and told them what my desire was. They were glad to hear the proposal to organize a Church of that denomination. A number of persons gave their names as members and wished to establish a permanent church; but they had no house in which to worship. They resolved to build one, and for the purpose of consulting about the matter they assembled together and agreed on a plan, and concluded to try it. They bought a lot on a respectable street and began to make necessary preparations for building." Though only serving in a local capacity, Early assisted in the work of construction.

In those days of hardships and inconveniences, men were not easily baffled in their pursuits. If they could not command money, they could labor with their hands. Early says, "When we repaired to the quarry for stone to lay the foundation, I was the first to open the earth and dig out a stone, they hauled it to the place and built the foundation with rejoicing, and the corner stone was laid in its proper place." The Church arose by means of great effort and much labor, and in due time African Methodism was established in that town also, and that church in after years became a flourishing station. It was the same in which Bishop Shorter was convicted and converted. Seeing the fruits of his labor so manifest, he says, "I was filled with such zeal for the extension of the Church that no difficulties or obstacles could turn me from my course. Though my home was in St. Louis, and my family resided there, my business often called me to other cities, and frequently to those at a great distance from the one in which I lived, I never failed to make an effort to establish our favorite Church wherever I went.

"About the year 1842 I had business which caused me to spend much time in the city of New Orleans. While there I saw the need of an African Methodist Church being established. The people were intelligent and desired to improve their condition, but were much hampered by oppression and proscriptive laws, and needed the stimulating influence of just such a Church, because it carried with it the spirit of progress. It declared that God is our father and man our equal and not our oppressor, and it taught the laws of self-government. They asked no man's permission where or how they should worship God, but they worshiped him according to his own word."

Early says, "I began to ponder in my mind how my designs might be accomplished. I frequently asked God to give me light on the subject and direct my course so that I could not fail to use the right methods to reach the end I so much desired. Hope sprang up in my heart as I pursued the matter further, though the prospect seemed gloomy at its first conception. I was closely allied to a number of men who were members of the masonic fraternity. My mind led me to confer with them on the utility of making the effort to start a church of that kind. They agreed to try the project, provided permission could be obtained from the state authorities. Brother James Hunter, a man of worth and integrity, had a friend who was a member of the Legislature of the State of Lousiana. He prevailed on that friend to bring a bill before that body, asking permission to establish an African Methodist Episcopal Church. It passed that such should be established for free people of color, provided they should meet at any hour between sunrise and sunset. No meetings could be held in any colored church after sunset. They secured a charter under those restrictions, and I commenced immediately to draw the people together. The incorporation was given to the African Methodist Episcopal Church, and under that name the people gladly assembled, both bond and free, to sing and pray and hear exhortations. We were obliged to meet in private houses and that with great caution. We often had to conceal ourselves from the police, meeting in an obscure room as far back from the streets as possible, and keep a watchman on duty near the opening of the alley, so that he might send a signal back to us and we might be able to disperse without being detected. No one who has only lived in the present generation can form the least conception of the terrors and disquietudes which the colored people experienced who lived in the slave holding states. That nefarious system of human oppression aimed to crush out all the light of the human soul. It made no compromise with wisdom or worth. All it called for was the utter subjection and degradation of the man-- soul, body and spirit, in consequence of which there was a constant jealousy and suspicion exercised toward free colored people, for fear that they might diffuse some practical knowledge among the slaves or excite them to desire freedom, which seemed to overshadow their minds with a constant dread and apprehension of evil. We were always under the ban of the law. They kept the patrol, who were like thirsty bloodhounds on the track of human security, ever present with us, and those who were most intelligent among us were compelled to resort to many devices to evade their intended cruelty. Thus the years passed on and our numbers increased until they were too numerous to be accommodated in private quarters, and we began to think about providing better accommodations. Our proceedings were watched with the utmost vigilance on all sides by the slaveholders and other enemies of the infant Church, for fear that we might make some innovations on their old and settled usages. We were often threatened with terrible penalties if we did not desist from our course. But we trusted in God, believing that he was stronger than man, and pressed forward against all opposing forces."

Says Early, "And the liberty and satisfaction I felt in exhorting and leading that precious band forward amply repaid me for all my toil. After a number of years had passed we began to make preparations to build a house of worship. We purchased a piece of ground on Romer street, on which we erected a beautiful house, which was dedicated 'St. James Chapel.' While all this was transpiring, so great was the hostility of the members of other churches exercised against us, who constantly endeavored to stir up the public by circulating false reports, I was often compelled to conceal myself through the week to avoid personal violence or the penalties of the law, and would repair to the church on Sabbath and preach to the people, because they had no authority to arrest us on the Sabbath. Finally through the course of years of difficulties and trials, we were enabled to triumph over all obstacles, and the membership now was sufficiently large to sustain a pastor, and Brother Charles Doughty was installed as such in the year 1847.

"At this distant period when I look back over those years of danger and toil, I wonder at the amazing goodness of God, who, amidst the protestations and invectives of such implacable enemies, did by the strength of his Almighty hand and the tenderness of his mercies, protect us from their wrath and lead us safely by the still waters of consolation, till we, with the crown of success encircling our brow, could exclaim, 'Victory,' in the name of Him who has saved us by grace. I am filled with wonder at the courage that was granted to us--that we in the face of the cruel magistrates of the law and the bloody whipping post and torture of the lash and the deathlike grip of the stocks, could with undaunted courage go forward.

"There is one circumstance that assisted me much. I was acquainted with many respectable citizens and became quite intimate with some who were more compassionate than others. These often interfered in our behalf and screened us from the vile intentions of our enemies. This work being finished, I was called and repaired to other parts of the Master's vineyard, blessing God that I had been counted worthy to labor in his holy cause."

He says, further, in commenting on these times of hardships and trials, "I cannot forget those brethren who labored with me in building up the cause of African Methodism: Brother Robert Martial, Brothers James Boyd and James Harris, of St. Louis, Mo., and Brother Doughty and others, of New Orleans; so godly, so vigilant, so zealous, always abounding in the work of the Lord. Though they are all long since gone to their rest, their memory still lingers with me, and their works of love and words of cheer will follow me till the end of my mortal existence.

"I could now see the hand of God directing me in my course as a local preacher, while the churches were in an infant state and struggling for existence. Not able to employ regular pastors, they could only get preaching as they could find now and then men who were kind enough to sympathize with their condition. Sometimes an Episcopalian would furnish them a sermon, and sometimes men of other denominations would preach; but the local preachers were always ready for every good word and work. I found myself adapted to this work, for I could carry on my secular business, and also attend to the work which devolved upon a local preacher. It was a work that I felt an especial call to perform. To exhort and pray and preach and stimulate the flock and keep up the regular meetings and ward off the assaults of the many enemies of the Church, was my highest delight and most sacred duty."

CHAPTER V.

"Our Church wherever established was called an abolition church, which made the slaveholders suspicious of its proceedings, and sometimes the members and local preachers were brought before courts of justice to answer for the absence of some slave who had made his escape. At one time, in the year 1846, some enemy of the cause reported that I knew something about some persons who were missing. I was called before the grand jury to answer to the charge. The foreman asked me what I knew about the 'underground railroad.' I asked him to explain what it was, for I never had seen a railroad underground. He said that it was 'Abolition.' Then I asked what he thought 'abolition' meant; and he said, *'Stealing niggers!'* I told him I thought 'abolition' meant to abolish or to put an end to anything. I told him that I did not steal. If I did, I would certainly steal myself first. Then he asked me what I would do if I saw one running away. I told him I would give him a dollar and tell him to run with all his might! The last answer seemed to amuse them, and finding they could elicit nothing from me I was released. I knew that I was in a critical condition, for if it could be proven that any man assisted in the least one who was making his escape, the punishment would be very severe.

"About these times the laws of Missouri were such that no man could transact business in any part of the state or city, unless he were a citizen or had a permit from proper authorities. Bishop Payne had occasion to visit the church in St. Louis, but had failed to obtain the proper authority from the city officers. The enemies of African Methodism, who were always on the alert, had him arrested and brought before a magistrate. We employed an attorney for him, a Mr. Shreeves, who was a shrewd lawyer. He was indicted, but the name was given "Tom Payne," instead of Daniel A. Payne, from which fact his lawyer contended that he was not the man, and he was released. The lawyer told me to take him immediately, for he was my man. I hurried him out of court and put him into my carriage. I had a swift horse, and if ever a horse was made to travel, my horse did that day. We crossed the ice on the Mississippi, for it was winter, and landed him safely in the State of Illinois, in the house of Mrs. Priscilla Baltimore, where he was out of danger.

"After years of constant and hopeful labor we were made truly glad to see abundant fruit the proceeds of our labor. African Methodism being fully established in St. Louis, it extended its influence through the surrounding communities. The church established at New Orleans had won the attention of many parts of the South, and the work was fast spreading. About the year 1851, I began to think of the itinerant work. I thought seriously and prayerfully over the matter and asked for God's direction, that he might assist me in making my decision. I finally concluded to extend the missionary work through St. Louis county, and for some distance around in adjoining counties. I visited Carondelet, about eight miles from the city. I gathered the people together and made known to them my intentions. I set forth the doctrines of the A. M. E. Church and urged the utility of forming a society of that persuasion. They accepted the offer and we formed a mission with twenty-five members. We then organized a church and appointed a leader and other officers. The people were glad, and thanked God for the advent of a Church which guaranteed to them so much religious liberty. They prayed earnestly and their number grew, and their meetings were the source of much good."

Early was diligent in his work, and the organization became permanent, and the church grew into a station in after years, with its trustees, stewards and leaders, and a permanent Sabbath-school attached to it. Rev. Moses Dixon was its first regular pastor. It then met in a rented house, but the members were not satisfied with such scanty quarters. They soon rallied their numbers and purchased a piece of ground, the very spot which they were then renting, and built an excellent church.

"The next place that I visited was Kirkwood, Missouri, a town about twelve miles from the city of St. Louis. This was in 1853. There I organized a church with ten or twelve members. They formed a class and started a regular prayer meeting. These means of grace had a tendercy not only to strengthen the membership, but they placed a strong incentive before others of like persuasion, until their members increased sufficiently to warrant a permanent organization. They elected trustees, appointed stewards and leaders, and organized a Sabbath-school, in which to instruct their young people in the truths of the Gospel. In course of time they built themselves a good, substantial edifice in which to worship God.

"The first place I visited and established a church was at St. Charles on the Missouri river. The next was Roach Port. In both places these organizations became permanent, and was the means of accomplishing much good.

"In each of the above named places our labors were blessed to the conversion of many souls, some of whom in a short time passed safely through the valley and shadow of death, and found their rest in the bright realms of everlasting day.

"The next place in which I introduced African Methodism was Washington, Missouri. I there called the people together and organized a church in a private house; but the people hearing of the advent of our Church into the city, came together in such numbers that we were obliged to obtain the court house in which to hold our meetings. We worshiped there until the membership was strong enough to build a church, which they accomplished in a short time, and became a permanent station with a salaried pastor, and it was the means of salvation to many souls."

There is something remarkable about the independence seen in the pioneer builders of the A. M. E. Church. The infant churches belonging to large bodies received financial help from the Mother Church; but these seldom asked or received help from any source. They seemed to rely entirely on their own efforts, sustained by the power of God.

The next point Early visited, was Jefferson City, Missouri, in 1853. Here as in all other places when African Methodism was introduced, they could find no public place in which to worship. They were obliged to resort to private houses, as Paul did in the city of Rome. A good brother, who was deeply interested in the work, opened his doors and they gladly accepted the opportunity. He says, "I gathered as many people together as I could find and formed a class consisting of ten or twelve members, and appointed a leader to conduct the meetings, and also appointed regular prayer meetings which were well attended. The young people were very fond of our ordinances and were present at all times. The Sabbath-school was well attended and the church membership was soon large enough to erect a church. They employed a regular pastor. In time it became a station."

CHAPTER VI.

In all the efforts of early Methodism the class meetings had a peculiar fascination about them which accompanied no other means of grace. They were then held with closed doors and persons would often accompany their friends who belonged to the church, and stand about the house in which they were assembled, and listen with intense eagerness to catch, if possible, a single word that might be spoken within doors, and would listen with rapt attention to the songs that were sung so full of life and power. Many persons date their conviction and conversion to these sacred influences. African Methodism carried with it a remarkably stimulating influence to incite people to grasp after a greater amount of intelligence. Wherever a church was organized a Sabbath-school was sure to follow. A well sustained day school would spring up and industry and thrift were discernible on all sides among the people.

"The next place I visited," Early says, "was Louisiana, Pike County, Missouri. There the people seemed to be waiting for the summons to enlist in the Army of the Lord, under the banner of African Methodism. The people rallied to the standard and we organized a church which stands to-day, where the faithful continue to meet to worship God. Then I crossed the great Missouri and organized in Boonville, Missouri. There with the usual readiness and joy the people came together and joined in praise and prayer to God. I always found an earnest few who were anxiously looking for the incoming of the kingdom of Christ. That select number I found here. They united in a church, and many soon joined their ranks, and in course of a short time they had a strong mission, and many rejoiced in the new found love of Christ their Redeemer. This mission, too, soon built themselves a place to worship and had a regular pastor. In St. Joseph, Missouri, I established a mission attended with the usual success, which, with the energy of the people sustained by the mercies of God, in a short time became a strong and active church. I visited Weston on the Missouri river and there established a mission which grew and prospered, and in the course of time was the means of the salvation of many souls." The difficulties which the pioneer ministers encountered are not known to or experienced by the ministers of the present day.

Early says, "When I first entered into the mission field of the A. M. E. Church, we had no stations or circuits in the West, and not even houses in which to worship."

In all the slave states oppression and prejudice were at their height of power. Strong and bitter enemies assailed us on every side, and dangers awaited them continually; for there were no means of travel except on horseback or on foot. There were very few bridges over the rivers, and often while fording the streams on horses, the Christian travelers would be nearly submerged by water; yet they were undaunted, and counted it all joy to suffer for their Master's cause. For God sustained and comforted them. But, Oh! how times have changed. We can sing our loud hallelujahs without being watched by sentinels, or reported to magistrates, or incarcerated in prisons.

"The years had rolled along from 1833, when I first was licensed to exhort, till it was approaching the year 1851. Through the decade from 1840 to 1850 I labored incessantly in the mission work, though most of the time in a local capacity, supporting and educating my family without aid from the churches. Now I come with many trophies to lay at the Master's feet. I had been ordained deacon for some years. In the year 1853 I thought of entering fully into the itinerant work which would be to me better vantage ground to prosecute the battle so successfully begun. When I looked back over the labors which I had passed through, I could but exclaim, 'What hath God wrought through an instrument of clay'--so many churches standing as monuments of God's mercies, and a membership increased from a persecuted few, scattered here and there, to thronging thousands, mostly of sober, respectable people. I rejoiced not only that my work had not been in vain, but that the cause which I so much loved was widening and deepening in all directions. The mountains of the East echoed with the glad song of the redeemed, while the prairies of the West were resonant with God's praise.

"God had, as I always believed, directed my course through the many years that I had struggled along in the ministry, striving to mark out a pathway for the advancement of that great and powerful Church which should so soon extend itself over the land, gathering in so many thousands of the oppressed sons and daughters of Africa. I now felt safe in believing that he was now moving on my heart to enter the itinerant ranks. Accordingly I arranged my business with an idea of taking the field. The missionaries had widened the boundaries of the Church in every direction, and many of the states had received African Methodism, and large circuits were formed in Illinois, Indiana, Missouri, and other states. A great many missions had been established in Missouri, Louisiana, Kentucky, Arkansas and Mississippi. Conferences had been held in the State of Indiana, whose jurisdiction extended over Missouri, Illinois and Kentucky. In these Conferences the missionary question was freely discussed, and a committee appointed to look after its condition. The temperance question also received some attention, for the Discipline of the Church discarded the use of strong drink among its members. The Sabbath-schools were made a necessary appendage of the Church, and the question received much attention in the Conferences. There were many resolutions passed on these important topics, after which many enlightening discussions would follow. In the year of 1853 or 1854 I entered the traveling list under the auspices of the Indiana Conference. Sometime afterwards I was sent to Chester Circuit, Ill., where I took in Sparta and all the region round. On this circuit I found much work to do, and much good followed."

Early says in performing these arduous duties for which he had no precedent: "I had such firm trust in God that I had no thought of failing. 'Onward,' was my motto, through every opposition until the appointed work was finished."

CHAPTER VII.

The perilous times of the civil war were now approaching, and it was both dangerous and difficult to travel in the Southern and Western states, even with a pass from the chief military officers of the district.

"About the year 1861 I was appointed to the Shawneetown Circuit, Ill., which consisted of six counties. The appointments were numerous, but each one was filled every two weeks. This arrangement required me to preach every day, and often two or three times a day. I was accustomed to ride thirty or forty miles a day to reach an appointment to be filled at night, stopping often to preach by the way and then hurrying on so as to reach my evening meetings to preach to an overflowing congregation. The horrors and dangers of the civil war were then to be encountered and it required an unusual amount of courage and boldness for any man to be able to go through the country on any errand."

Early says at one time while on his circuit there was a mob raging through the surrounding district, which assailed many of the colored people, beating some and wounding others. This treatment brought on a conflict between the two parties and two of the mob were killed and a number more were wounded. The next day, not knowing what had happened, he went to his appointment. The best of the citizens knew to what danger he would be exposed. A number of them mounted their horses and surrounded the church and guarded it until the meeting was over. So he escaped unhurt.

A short time afterward, he says it was reported that he was a fugitive from slavery, with live hundred dollars reward offered for his arrest and delivery to the proper authorities. He says: "While on the road to my appointment I was overtaken by a man who insisted that I was a runaway slave and desired me to surrender immediately. I told him I would not, but I accompanied him back some miles to a magistrate where I found a number of men assembled who bore the most formidable aspect. They insisted on my being detained and held for proof of my identity. I told them that they did not dare to detain me without a warrant from an officer of the government. The magistrate agreed with me. I knew that they were well armed and would give me trouble if they could get me into their power; but while they went out to regale themselves with a fresh drink, I gave the squire the sign of the Masonic fraternity, which he acknowledged, and I showed him my papers both from the government and my native state. He immediately refused to have anything more to do with me, so after I had been delayed several hours I went on my way and reached my appointment in time to preach to a large assembly at night." He further says, "There were great revivals in those years of trials and danger. Such outpourings of the spirit of God as I have never seen before or since. Hundreds of souls were converted to God and brought into the church and often for days together in many places their shouts and songs of praise could be heard far and near while they continued together singing and praying and listening to the dispensation of the words of life. Surely God was with us. We have been made to feel that the good influences of this work will never cease while memory lasts or time endures. My year's labor came to a close, and I repaired to the Annual Conference which met in St. Paul St. Louis. We had an interesting time, at the close of which I received my appointment from Bishop Quinn to St. Louis circuit. The work was accompanied with the usual circumstances of building up missions, but I kept constantly at work. A number of members were added to the church and the societies though small, were lively and active. I paid much attention to Sabbath-schools, bringing in not only the children of the members, but as many of the young men and women for helpers as I could persuade to come from the surrounding community. In so doing we secured many members for the church that we could not have obtained otherwise. The year passed on and the influence of our Church extended further each month. The Conference for 1864 was drawing nigh. It was to meet in St. Louis, and I prepared my report of the work done. We met and with joy rehearsed the many fought battles and the many victories won. The session was an interesting one. The various committees reported and discussions followed. The committee on Temperance, State of the Country, Education, and Missions were all handled with much interest. The business of the Conference being finished we all prepared for our departure. The Conference was presided over by Bishop W. P. Quinn, and I was sent to Carondelet Circuit. I entered on my work with renewed vigor. The people gave me their confidence, for I had labored with them previous to this time. I found the membership to be over one hundred. They were lively and active and faithful in the performance of their duty. I labored incessantly to build up the work in the church and to spread its influence as far as possible. My desire was gratified to some extent. I lived to see churches spring up in every direction through the State and circuits formed in many places."

"In September, 1865, we repaired to St. James Chapel, New Orleans, to attend the Annual Conference presided over by Bishop J. P. Campbell. The brethren came together bearing with them good tidings of their past year's labor. They had won many trophies for their Master. This Conference was conducted in an earnest and lively manner, many things being considered which were intended to advance our future interest. In those days when the advantages for education were few the ministers were required to engage in as much private study as was compatible with their other duties, and to bring in a written article on some specified topic, to be read and criticised by the Bishop and Conference. This they found to be a great means of improving their minds. There were many such read before this Conference on a certain day appointed for the purpose. The discussions following were instructive and interesting in the highest degree. I served as one of the committee on the subject of. Missions, and our chairman made a lively and interesting report. The Temperance question was discussed and the ministers were required to preach a sermon during the course of the year on that especial topic. Education was a theme of much interest and the ministers were required to do all in their power to enlighten their own minds and to encourage the building up of schools. This very interesting session of Conference finally came to a close, and the ministers, with many thanks to the good people of New Orleans, prepared to take their departure to their several appointments. My own assignment was to Asbury Chapel, Louisville, Kentucky. I was now called upon to bid farewell to the scenes I loved so dearly, and take my departure to a new and untried field of labor. The churches in Missouri and Illinois and Louisiana were dear to me, not only because I had spent so many years of faithful labor among them, but it was while with them I received the unction that had sustained me and urged me forward so long. In St. Louis I was converted, and there I received license to exhort in the year 1833.

"In the Missouri Conference I was licensed to preach the everlasting gospel of Christ. I had while a member of the Indiana Conference received the holy orders of deacon in the year 1840, and afterward while in the Missouri Conference I was ordained elder in the year 1846 by Bishop Payne. I had built up many missions which were now organized into stations and circuits, and were represented in the Annual Conferences. In St. Louis I had entered into the family relation and there after years of happy consort I had laid my dear wife in the grave. All these hallowed associations I was now called upon to leave."

CHAPTER VIII.

"In the year 1865 I took charge of Asbury Chapel in Louisville, Kentucky, which was then under the supervision of the Missouri Conference. It was a well-appointed station and had an active membership numbering two hundred. The people were pleased with my administration and filled the church to overflowing the most respectable people of color in the city attending at each service. The church enjoyed a continual revival, and its numbers increased rapidly, and in the course of the year the membership almost doubled itself, and African Methodism enjoyed much favor from all classes of the citizens. The Sabbath-school, under the leadership of an efficient superintendent, grew in numbers weekly and received much favor from the people who sent in their children from every quarter. The young people built up a fine choir. The classes were diligent and fervent, and every department of the work proceeded in the utmost harmony. These were in the midst of the most troublesome times, just after the close of the civil war, and the hostilities between the different sections had scarcely ceased; but the hand of the good Lord was leading us, and his power protecting us, and those who had seemed to be our most uncompromising enemies became our friends, and the year passed off without incidents from that quarter.

"But in the midst of all this prosperity and the endearments with which I was surrounded, I was called upon in the month of October, 1866, to repair to the Annual Conference which would convene in St. Paul Chapel, St. Louis, Missouri, presided over by Bishop J. P. Campbell. The cholera was raging in that city at the time; but as faithful servants of God, no one seemed to fear the danger that attended their going. Each member came up with boldness and presented himself at the proper time and at the place appointed. The Conference opened its session at the appointed hour and all the members answered to the roll call. But the dreaded intruder had hurled his shaft at one of their number, and the angel of death spread his dark wings over that consecrated body and bore from their number their much loved friend and brother, Austin Woodfork. After a very solemn but pleasant and interesting session, the appointments were announced for the following year. I was much surprised to know that I was assigned to South Nashville, Tennessee. It was a hard trial for me to leave my beloved station with such bright prospects before me for future success. But the Master had called and I conferred not with my own inclinations, but proceeded immediately to obey the summons. I bade farewell to my beloved congregation, settled up my business, and took my departure. Arriving at the mission I immediately called the people together and preached my first sermon from Acts x. 29: 'I ask therefore for what intent ye have sent for me?' It is impossible at this date to conceive what effect it had on the people. Every heart seemed to respond to the question of the great Apostle, and the whole Church of Nashville seemed to arouse to immediate action. To South Nashville Mission were attached eleven counties viz: Davidson, Rutherford, Bedford, Coffee, Sumner, Trousdale, Warren, Wilson, Maury and Giles, to visit all of which it was necessary to travel several hundred miles. In some of those counties there had been no A. M. E. Church established. In South Nashville there had been a number of members drawn off from the whites, and Elder Woodfork had charge of them a part of the previous year. They were then meeting with much opposition so that they could make but slow advancement; yet they were not discouraged, for their faces were toward the future, and their hands and hearts were lifted toward heaven and their confidence was placed in God.

"After various efforts to obtain a permanent place in which to worship and being sadly disappointed, for in some instances they had been badly treated, the little band concluded to attempt to obtain a place that they might call their own in which to worship. They bargained for a lot near the corner of South Cherry and Franklin Streets, at the enormous price of $7,500, and had not a cent in the treasury with which to make a payment. Their situation seemed to be discouraging indeed. But they had strong energy and high hopes. They were possessed of willing minds and ready hands, and they had faith to believe that some day they would obtain the required money. They then bought an old frame which had been used in time of war for a soldiers' mess house. It stood near by the lot and they proposed to move it on it and fit it up for a church. And thus I found the situation when I came. I saw immediately that there was a fine prospect for building up a good and permanent church. I called the members together and proceeded to organize according to Discipline. I had trustees elected, appointed stewards, arranged the classes, and established regular prayer meetings, with the most suitable men we could obtain for leaders of the same. As soon as this was done we began to make arrangements to repair the house. We turned it around laid a floor and had the walls plastered and had lamps hung and seats put in sufficient to accommodate several hundred people, and had it dedicated by the name of St. Paul Chapel. Then we commenced to hold our regular meetings by preaching three times on Sabbath. The congregation grew so rapidly that it was necessary to put an addition to the house so as to seat the constantly growing audience. When the proposition was made, the church unanimously went to work. Both men and women seemed to vie with each other as to which should do the most in collecting funds. The addition was soon completed and the church would then accommodate one thousand persons. There was then great rejoicing and the spiritual work went on and grew and prospered daily. There was a continual revival. So much so that no Sabbath passed without receiving a number of persons into the church, and there were persons baptized almost every Sabbath. This condition of spiritual enjoyment continued for about three years, in which time I received into the church 996 members, all of whom were baptized and regularly enrolled on the class books."

Early introduced the weekly prayer meetings, general class meetings, the first Sabbath in each month, and monthly communions, which drew the people from every quarter and filled the house with eager worshipers. The Sabbath-school was attended by more than four hundred scholars each Sabbath. Many persons from the suburban villages joined this church, but the distance was too far for them to attend their weekly classes regularly. "After consulting with the brethren and praying over the matter, we concluded to establish a branch church in Edgefield, now East Nashville. In the latter part of the year 1867, we found a lot on Bass street, with a house that suited us, which we purchased for $1,500. We organized a church, took possession of the house, repaired it and placed over it Rev. Timothy Burton as it pastor. The house was afterward dedicated under the name of Payne's Chapel. From about twenty members it has now become one of our first stations. In the year 1868 we organized a church in West Nashville with about ninety members which we named Bethel, dedicated it, and placed as pastor over it, the Rev. Henry Glassgo. This church has since then built a substantial brick edifice, and is now a thriving station. In South Nashville, in the year 1868, we organized a church with forty members. One of our friends donated a piece of ground on which we erected a brick house which was dedicated, Ebenezer Church. It has since become a station. Its first pastor was Rev. Charles Russel." In the meanwhile there were churches organized in all the counties, over which Early had charge. Houses of worship were erected suitable for the times, and the people gathered into them. The majority of those churches are now flourishing stations.

Early says, "Besides my arduous work in the churches in the city, I generally made it convenient to spend every third Sabbath in some one of those eleven counties. It was quite a difficult matter to reach many parts of the state, there being few railroads, and only a small number of places could be reached by them. The common roads everywhere being in a bad condition, the traveling was necessarily done on horseback or in rough wagons, through mountainous parts where there were no turnpikes or leveled roads, besides many dangerous rivers to cross."

CHAPTER IX.

"The hostilities occasioned by the civil war had not ceased, and persons were questioned and often threatened with violence when they were passing quietly along. The 'Ku Kluxs' were numerous in the country, and the people were frequently interrupted when attempting to gather together. A collision would often occur between the two parties, in which persons would sometimes be wounded or killed, and that would create much sensation, and sometimes trouble would follow. At one time when in Bedford County holding meetings, the 'Ku Kluxs' assailed a colored family in their own house. The father of the family shot one of the men, at which they were greatly enraged and vowed vengeance on any one they should meet. It was on Saturday when this occurred, and I was lodging within a mile or two of the place. Sabbath morning came and all my friends were afraid for me to preach. But I started boldly for the church. When I had almost reached it a number of men came riding up. I dismounted went in and commenced the service, praying all the while that God would protect me. Before I concluded my sermon they retired.

"In Shelbyville, Tenn., the Southern Methodists gave us a church which would hold about three hundred persons. We accepted the gift, and placed in charge Rev. Jeremiah Bowman, who was very successful in his labors. The church increased in interest until it became a station. We established a church at Wartrace and at Macedonia. A pastor named Jefferson Mackelroy, came over to us with all his members, numbering four hundred persons. When we convened our first quarterly conference at Shelbyville, Tenn., fifty local preachers presented themselves for work. These were of the number recently taken in. Many of those brethren were warm and zealous speakers, and had rendered much help in the Church. A number of them were presented to the Annual Conference for ordination. Bishop Campbell protested that he would ordain no man who could neither read nor write. But after we had explained to him how much their help was needed, he consented to lay his hands upon them and to send them into the field. All of them proved themselves to be worthy followers of their Master, until called from labor to reward.

"The end of the Conference year began to approach, and all prepared themselves to attend the Annual Conference which was to convene in August, 1867, in St. Paul Chapel, Nashville, Tenn. Bishop J. P. Campbell presided. Great preparations were made to entertain Tennessee's first Annual

Conference of the A. M. E. Church. The people flocked in from every quarter, and we had an interesting and profitable time. There was much rejoicing at the unparalleled prosperity of the A. M. E. Church. There were a number of ministers presented for admission who were accepted and admitted for orders. They were ordained on the third Sabbath in August, 1867, with impressive ceremonies. The reports from the different parts of the State were encouraging in the highest degree. Circuits had been formed and traveled and presided over by efficient and energetic men. There were a number of churches which had grown large enough to be denominated stations. These were given regular salaried pastors. The missionary work was extending the church in different parts of the State, and from that work was reported many conversions, and a large number of members brought into the fold. Great interest had been taken in establishing Sabbath-schools, the members of which numbered 1,876. The total membership for St. Paul was 519; of the church, 1,671. The temperance question received some attention, and much was said on the propriety of the ministers being sober. At the close of the Conference, I was appointed to St. Paul for the second time to serve them as their pastor, while the work was being pushed forward in South and East Nashville. Rev. Basil Brooks, who was stationed at St. John, which he had established, was doing valiant work for the Master's cause. St. John Chapel, under his wise administration, had become a flourishing station, and St. James, and Salem Chapel, which he organized in North Nashville, were doing well. Our work for the second year was very peaceful and prosperous, all our opponents being silenced by our quiet vigilance in all our religious matters. African Methodism being firmly established in the State, we entertained no further fears for its future safety.

"I had time to devote to our further improvement. I went to the gas company and bargained with them to put gas pipes from the main one into the church, which greatly improved our condition by having the church properly lighted. Then I began to think of introducing a choir into the church. I often called the young people together for the purpose of practicing what music they then understood. In the course of the year they formed a choir which sang in the church. Through the course of the next year they purchased an organ, and Mrs. Molly Tuggle was the first organist. She held the place for a time and was then succeeded by Miss Mary A. Watson, who has held it ever since.

"The Conference year came to a close, and on the 10th of September, 1868, the Annual Conference met in St. John Chapel, Nashville, Tennessee. When the members assembled and gave in their reports, we found that it had been a year of great success in all parts of the district. Bishop J. A. Shorter presided with his usual ability. The committees on missions, temperance, and state of the country, gave good reports. The membership was not so large this year, because so many persons had removed out of the stations to other cities and also to the country. St. Paul gave in one thousand one hundred and eight members, six preachers, nine exhorters and four churches. I was Conference treasurer that year, besides serving on several committees. The Conference came to a close, and I was reappointed to St. Paul Chapel."

CHAPTER X.

"I took hold of the work in my charge with renewed vigor, for it was my third and last year. I had attended the General Conference, which met in Washington, D. C., in May of that year, and was much encouraged by its proceedings, and refreshed by conversation with many of my former comrades in the Gospel. When I looked at the work before me, I was astonished at its advancement. There had been many elders and deacons ordained and sent out on the circuits so that I was relieved of much of my former work. I had only three missions to preside over, Franklin, Goodlettsville and Hartsville, besides my own charge. We had up to this time been able to pay the interest on the church debt, but there had been so many repairs and other expenses to meet that we had not as yet been able to replenish the treasury. All this time I had been schooling the people up to a higher plain of action. We had then a model Sabbath-school, which numbered six hundred and seventy-three pupils--these were in regular attendance.

"September 1, 1869, we met in Avery Chapel, Memphis, Tenn. The Conference was presided over by Bishop J. A. Shorter, and was large and well attended. The people of the different churches and denominations showed a deeper interest than usual in its proceedings, there being large crowds present at every session. All the business of the Conference was transacted with the utmost harmony, and peace and good will seemed to prevail among the brethren. How strong the A. M. E. Church had become in so short a time! We were convinced, as good Dr. Revels often said, that it was 'A child of heaven rocked in the bosom of God,' and that it was leading our people, both spiritually and morally, to a higher plain of action and giving them a spirit of independence not otherwise known to them.

"I took charge of A very Chapel under the most favorable circumstances. The membership numbered eight hundred and seventy; preachers, seven; exhorters, five. The Sabbath-school reported two hundred and sixty scholars. The church was engaged in a series of prayer meetings, which were lively and earnest. The people came together in great numbers and a revival of religion commenced, in which there were more than one hundred conversions. The congregation was generally larger than the house could accommodate. There were seldom less than a thousand present on Sabbath evenings, and very often more. The membership increased daily, and the classes were overflowing. There were about eighteen, and they always rendered a good report. The young people of all classes came in freely and assisted in all the services. I soon saw the necessity of a good choir. I obtained a good musical director and had a class well trained for the purpose. We constructed seats for them, bought an organ, obtained an organist, and introduced the choir to the church. All were pleased and the community was very grateful for their services.

"The church building I found greatly in need of repair. I called the officers together and consulted them about the best means to raise the money for the needed work. We agreed upon a plan and laid it before the members. They agreed to do their best in raising the means. They contributed freely, and all the friends of the church assisted with a will. The money was soon obtained, and the repairing was done."

Early says, "I was always a lover of light, so I could not rest until I had the church lighted with gas. I brought the matter before the church and they agreed to it and we had the fixtures put in the house and the gas turned on.

In the year 1870, there was a stirring revival in the church. Day and night the meetings went on and many were converted and added to the church. They were baptized and enrolled on the class books. The Sabbath-school continued to increase and the various benevolent societies of the church flourished and were strong. Several of the young men who had recently professed religion felt that they were called of God to preach the Gospel, and soon applied to their classes for recommendations to the quarterly conference for license. They, of course, being found blameless in life and conversation obtained their desire. These, added to some other local preachers already in the church, made a very strong force to do good. Besides assisting in the ordinances of the church, they did good missionary work in the surrounding country. Prayer meetings were frequent and conducted with great zeal, the women bearing their part with no less ardor than the men. Surely the presence of the Lord was with us continually, and warmed every earnest heart with heavenly fire. Whenever those sainted women poured out their souls to God in their accustomed eloquent and fervent strains, the Holy Ghost seemed to be almost visible. The membership was so large that there was a great amount of pastoral work to be done. Visiting the sick, burying the dead, performing the marriage ceremony, and the daily calls of those persons who wished to obtain advice and for conversation and prayer, made the work arduous in the extreme; but God was with us and gave us strength in every emergency and comfort in every hour of trial.

"About the close of the year 1870, the laboring force of the church became so strong that I began to cast about for some needy section where we might establish a permanent church, and thus glorify God by the extension of his kingdom.

"Our co-workers were doing valiant work in different parts of the city: Rev. B. Williamson at St. Andrew, and Brother R. Tally, at Central Point; but these churches though large and influential did not cover all the ground. There was much effort needed in other directions. After asking help of God to show us the proper place, we found that the Second Adventists in Chelsea, a suburban village, were about to offer their church for sale. We concluded at once that this was intended to be an answer to our prayers. We notified the trustees of Avery Chapel of the offer, and asked them to ascertain the price at which the church and grounds were offered for sale. They conferred with the owners, who agreed to take four thousand dollars ($4,000) for the whole premises. The trustees agreed to give them their price, provided they would give them the privilege of paying for it in different installments, to which they agreed and they made a payment, took possession of the church, organized an A. M. E. church, and placed over it as pastor, Rev. Breckenridge. The church was dedicated 'St. James Chapel,' by Bishop Shorter. The membership increased slowly, but permanently, so that in the course of time it became a flourishing station. Thus there were four A. M. E. stations in the city of Memphis. The pastors encouraged each other, being stimulated by mutual efforts to build up the kingdom of Christ and sustained by the grace of God. The cheerful acquiescence of the membership in everything we undertook to do, cannot be forgotten. Their fervent love and undying friendship sustained us under many trying circumstances, and raised our drooping spirits when cast down.

"I have often thought that there was something remarkable about the success of the pioneer ministers. Although there were none of them who claimed to be educated, their achievements in building up churches and the spread of the Gospel are unequaled by any of the ministers of the present day. They seemed to be men who were imbued with the Holy Spirit, and their words appeared to be accompanied by a divine unction from above. They seldom preached a sermon without a peculiar demonstration of the power of

God to save souls. Their zeal and earnestness, accompanied with a remarkable comprehension of the meaning of the word of God, gave such force to their utterances that they went straight to the heart of the hearer and produced immediate conviction. Again, for the most part, they were men of unquestioned piety. Their deportment and conversation were chaste and godly. People believed and trusted them as fathers, and their words had great power to convince men of their errors and sins and in turning them to righteousness."

CHAPTER XI.

And now, time with all its changes and variations is rapidly speeding on, unfolding all the mysteries of human events; and the customs and usages of society are changing as other generations succeed us in their onward march. Many of our comrades in the Christian warfare had lain down their armor and had entered into eternal rest, wearing the crown of the victor; others had taken their places, of less experience and physical endurance and less spirituality in their sermons and conversation. About this time there was a perceptible change in the character of the worship. There had been for some time most excellent schools established among the people. The fine arts were taught to some extent, and the people had availed themselves of these advantages. Many of the young people were good performers on instruments, and had acquired a considerable knowledge of the art of music. These formed the choirs in the different churches, and when their voices were accompanied by the music of instruments, the character of the worship was greatly changed. A higher form of church ordinances was developed, and refinement and elegance was attendant in the house of God. The boisterous, demonstrative mode gradually disappeared in most instances, and the worship became of a more rational and elevated character. The A. M. E. Church, as usual, seemed to be the first to lay hold of necessary reforms, such as monthly communions, general speaking meetings, the introduction of choirs and organs into the churches, lighting their churches with gas, holding religious concerts and Sabbath-school exhibitions, and other social gatherings which always accompany an exalted Christianity. The great mass of respectable young people always followed them and greatly swelled their numbers and increased their favor among the people.

"Murfreesborough, Tenn., was the place appointed to hold the Annual Conference in the year 1870, to be presided over by Bishop J. A. Shorter. I wound up my church reports for the year and repaired to the place appointed for the Conference. The Conference was visited by a number of the most notable men of the Church, such as Rev. B. T. Tanner, Dr. J. T. Jenifer, Henry J. Young and others. These brethren by their witty sallies and apt discussions in the Conference added greatly to the life and activity of the body. I reported that year: members, 1,011; preachers, 8; Sabbath-school, total, 650. There was also a strong petition sent up for my return, accompanied by the favor of the best people. The Conference passed off peaceably and profitably, and I was reappointed to A very Chapel, Memphis.

"With exalted hopes and high prospects, I for the second year took charge of A very Chapel, Memphis, Tenn., and commenced my labors with renewed vigor. Rev. Page Tyler was assigned to Phoenix Chapel; Brother Gilbert Algee to Providence Chapel; and Brother Robert Talley to St. James Chapel. The churches were all enjoying peace and prosperity, and seemed to enjoy to a great extent both the favor of God and man. The membership of A very Chapel had greatly increased and the congregation was generally larger than the house could accommodate, the membership itself numbering near twelve hundred.

"There were great revivals that year in all the churches, and hundreds were added to the fold of Christ. We conducted that of A very Chapel for more than three months with great success, and many prominent young men and women joined the church, and became useful members therein.

"There was something wonderful about the amity that existed between the pastors of the various branches of the Methodist and Baptist churches. They conversed freely together on all vital topics concerning the advancement of the churches and the building up of the Redeemer's kingdom on earth, and the general interest of our oppressed people. The membership attended each other's prayer meetings, revival seasons, class meetings, love-feasts and baptizings, and kept up a continual interchange of religious courtesies which always developed a feeling of relationship among God's people not otherwise to be experienced. Thus the year 1871 passed off busily and profitably, and the people began to show signs of worldly prosperity, and thrift and industry were visible on all sides. Besides the vast labor attendant on the pastorate of our own church, we assisted in raising the payment on St. James Chapel, which they were then purchasing, and we also established a mission near Wolf River, into which many precious souls were gathered. This mission was presided over by Rev. William Armor, a man of great religious zeal and perseverance, who also had charge of another mission on one of the islands of the Mississippi River, which was near by."

The influence of African Methodism was now being felt all through the state of Tennessee. Churches were being established and missions formed all through the Southern and Western parts of the state. Young men were daily entering into the ministry, and helpers were springing up in all departments of the Church, which greatly increased her working force and her power to enlarge her borders. Every year the Conference increased in numbers and constantly grew in dignity and intelligence.

In Tennessee Conference were then a number of the most powerful orators in the A. M. E. Connection, such as W. B. Revels, H. A. Jackson, B. L. Brooks, Page Tyler, all of whom might be termed "Sons of Thunder" in the pulpit, and of wide influence when out of it, and Pastors J. W. Early, Page Tyler, B. L. Brooks, and others, who have not been excelled in the field. But the year of 1871 was winding to a close, and we were admonished that it was time to make preparations for the Annual Conference, which was to meet in the city of Columbia, Tenn., on the 13th day of September, and would be presided over by Bishop James A. Shorter. We met at the appointed place and time. At the roll call there were seventy-one ministers who answered to their names, besides many visiting brethren from other Conferences, who took an active part. The brethren stood fair as to character and the committees were duly appointed. The missionary committee made a good report. Rev. J. W. Early was treasurer.

The reports from different parts of the state were highly satisfactory, and the older members of the Conference rejoiced greatly to see with their own eyes such abundant fruit produced in so short a time from the seed which they had scattered a few years previous. The precious seed which they had gone forth bearing with tears, had been gathered and returned with an increase of an hundred fold.

"I was returned from this Conference to Avery Chapel for my third and last year. All was in peace and prosperity, and the church was enjoying a reasonable portion of spiritual blessing. After making suitable arrangements for the winter, and adjusting the business of the church, with the consent of the brethren we deferred the revival meetings to the latter part of the winter. These meetings were largely attended and there were many conversions, and numbers were added to the church."

CHAPTER XII.

"We now began to make arrangements to attend the General Conference which was to be held the following May, 1872, in St. Paul Chapel, Nashville, Tennessee. I had been elected a delegate by the Annual Conference the previous fall. On the first Monday in May, 1872, we found ourselves assembled in the General Conference of the A. M. E. Church. There were great numbers present and the discussions were many and spirited. This Conference is memorable on account of the famous "Dollar Money System," which was introduced by Rev. H. J. Young. The bill was accepted by the Conference and went into effect as a law for all time thereafter. This was the last General Conference attended by the venerable and senior Bishop, Rt. Rev. William Paul Quinn, who after a life of the most arduous toil and wonderful endurance expressed himself as ready to lay down his armor and receive the crown. In his wonderful experience he had seen the advancement of the work beyond his utmost expectation.

With pathos, Bishop Quinn recalled the days of the poverty and weakness of the infant Church, and of their strong faith and ardent zeal in building up an institution which promised them the religious freedom they so much desired. The venerable Bishop expressed himself as satisfied with the advancement made by the Church in gaining favor with the world, and was astonished at its rapid growth. Being comparatively a handful at the beginning of his labors, and in the course of a lifetime it numbered its hundreds of thousands. He recalled the days when he had forded rivers, climbed mountains, crossed forests, encountered wild beasts, and faced and fought vindictive mobs, and was called before courts of justice to establish the Church he so much loved. He had in hunger and thirst and peril traveled thousands of miles to plant the Church in the West, and now his labors on earth were nearly ended. He bade his worthy colleagues who had labored and suffered with him, and whose heads were whitening with age, to be of good cheer and finish the fight of faith with unshaken confidence in God and soon they would meet and lay their trophies at the Saviour's feet.

"After the adjournment of General Conference we all returned to our labors with buoyant expectations of a bright and successful future. The congregation of Avery Chapel was now very large. The church had a seating capacity of about twelve hundred persons. It was always crowded on Sabbath evenings, and frequently great numbers were unable to gain admittance. That same year Elder Page Tyler, our worthy colleague and friend, began to build a new church for the congregation of Phoenix Chapel, now St. Andrew's Chapel. We rendered him all the assistance in our power; for it was always an especial trait of our church to extend a helping hand to each other whenever they were in need.

"My time at A very Chapel was now drawing to a close, and I began to prepare for another field of action. I settled up all the affairs of the church, laid in all the fuel for fires for the ensuing year, paid the gas bill for one year in advance, paid the insurance on the church property for the same length of time, and laid by in the treasury $1,300 to assist in purchasing a lot for the erection of a new church. September was approaching, on the 25th of which the Conference was to convene in Clarksville, Tenn., to be presided over by Bishop J. M. Brown. I bade adieu to the church I loved so much, and for whom I had labored and shared with them their joys and sorrows so long, and with many regrets and tears they gave me the parting hand and I repaired to the Annual Conference."

Says an eye witness of the last meeting that Early held in Memphis: "It was the largest congregation that I ever saw gathered at one church and such effusions of tears I had not seen shed at any one time. Their demonstrations of love were ratified by the number of presents and other manifestations tendered."

With happy greetings the brethren met in Conference, and joined in chorus and thanksgiving to God for his bountiful mercies through the past year. The number of traveling ministers was rapidly increasing, so that the membership of the Conference was very large. The discussions were lively and spirited, and sometimes the brethren were a little boisterous, but were soon brought to order by their dignified presiding officer, Bishop J. M. Brown. The reports for the year were good. The various resolutions gave signs of progress. Early says "I reported for the year 1872 of members, 1,500; Sabbath-school scholars 840; exhorters and preachers, 10; church extension, $1,300; dollar money, which was our first, $134."

"When the business of Conference was finished and we received our appointments, I was assigned to St. John's Chapel, Nashville Tenn., being elder in charge of the circuits of Brother Abram Moore, Brother Allen

Williams and Brother Alexander Winston. Rev. W. R. Revels, my colleague, was appointed to St. Paul Chapel.

"I took charge of this station under many depressing circumstances. The membership was divided, and many of them were not on good terms with each other. They had had many dissensions in the previous administration which had caused wounds that were hard to heal. The pastor had espoused the part of some, while he discarded that of others. These things stirred up much strife and bickerings, and seemed to check every effort to advance the cause of God. Besides all these things to contend with, there was a debt of long standing hanging over the church, for money which had been borrowed to pay for the ground on which the church was built. Many of the officers and members refused to make any efforts to raise the money to pay the debt, because they said that they had bargained to pay too much for the ground and their creditor was threatening to sue them unless they would make immediate effort to pay him. I saw that it was impossible to accomplish any good with so many incumbrances to hinder our efforts. So I called the officers together and consulted with them about some plan by which to raise the money to liquidate the debt. I told them that it was impossible to move forward with so much strife among us and so many accusations against us. I thought that the best way to bring the members on good terms with each other was to get them to work for their mutual benefit. When they were busy they would not think of strife, neither would their enemies carp if they were assured that they were making efforts to be honest. I urged them to try to get the business of the church into a more settled state, ere we could even ask God to bless our labors. We prayed and talked together, and finally decided on some plans that we thought would meet the approbation of the people, and proceeded to lay them before the church and congregation. When we did so every one seemed to be pleased with the prospect and declared themselves ready for action. Meanwhile the Sabbath-school began to increase and all things began to be enlivened.

"The majority of the membership went to work--some subscribing, others holding entertainments, and still others soliciting the public. So we gathered the money together with a readiness which astonished even ourselves, and in less than five months the debt of $1,300 was paid, and all the current expenses of the church beside. By this time general friendship prevailed in the church and there seemed to be a oneness of purpose in everything that we undertook to do. Our next object was to repair the church and light it with gas. This they readily consented to do. Each member who felt able and willing, subscribed a certain amount, and the windows and doors and walls were put in good order, the seats repaired and fastened down, the stoves righted up, and gas pipes run in and fixtures put in the church. All being finished, we commenced our protracted meetings, which were conducted with great harmony for some weeks. There was a glorious outpouring of the Spirit of God. There were more than one hundred conversions, ninety-seven of whom joined the church--fifty-two were immersed in the Cumberland river, the other forty-five were baptized around the altar. It was indeed a great time of rejoicing. During the year nearly one hundred others were received by letter and otherwise, which increased the members received to nearly two hundred."

CHAPTER XIII.

"In the spring of 1873 our city was visited by Asiatic cholera, that terrible scourge of mankind. The Angel of Death again spread his dark wings over our devoted city and touched with his sword-like hand the hearts of thousands of the citizens. A great number of our members were stricken down and borne to their graves. What was so remarkable of me was that I visited my members in every case, and I never felt the least symptons of the epidemic. God showed his love in protecting me from all harm in the midst of such danger.

"Many of our devoted members had gone to rest. They all died in the full triumphs of faith. The year 1873 was now coming to a close, and peace and prosperity had crowned our efforts. The classes were large and well attended, and the Sabbath-school had grown until there were more than five hundred names of scholars enrolled on the book.

"The Annual Conference was appointed to convene in St. Andrew's Chapel, Memphis, Tenn., September 24th, 1873. When the time came the yellow fever was raging so terribly that it was entremely dangerous to go near the city. But many of the brethren went boldly to the appointed place and reported at the opening hour. Bishop J. M. Brown, who was our presiding officer, did not make his appearance for some days. The brethren dispatched to him that they were waiting, and he answered them to go on with the Conference. They voted that Elder Page Tyler should take the chair, and the Conference was opened and they proceeded to business. The character of the ministers was examined, and all stood fair. None had been expelled and no one had withdrawn from the Connection. Three of their members had died that year, whom they trusted were at rest. The usual committees were appointed and all went into executive session.

"Bishop J. M. Brown arrived on the fourth day of the Conference and took possession of the chair. He explained why he delayed his coming so long. He had doubted whether it was expedient to expose the brethren to such imminent danger as they were in at that very hour by holding Conference at that place. A resolution was then offered that they would adjourn to meet at some future time to which they all agreed; but they still lingered.

"A resolution was then offered by Rev. R. F. Hurly, that the presiding elder system be adopted by the Tennessee Conference, and for which purpose a committee should be appointed to district the bounds of the Conference. The resolution provoked much discussion, but finally passed and became a law.

"On the sixth day of the Conference the epidemic had increased so alarmingly, that it was thought unwise to remain longer, so they adjourned to finish their business at St. John Chapel, Nashville, on October 24, 1873. The people were then dying so rapidly that coffins could not be procured fast enough to bury them.

"The Conference assembled at the appointed time in Nashville to complete its business. The reports of committees were received, the disbursements were made, and pastors and ministers made the returns of their year's work.

"St. John Chapel reported: Members, 536; preachers, 4; exhorters, 1; Sabbath-school scholars, 579; superintendents, 2. Salem Chapel, over which I had charge, was in a prosperous condition, under the care of Brother Aaron Young, as was also Mount Joliet Circuit, in charge of J. Griggs.

"The Annual Conference had steadily increased in numbers until there were more than fifty members present, and the field of labor had extended, until it now reached the greater part of the State. There was also a marked improvement in the efforts to enlighten and elevate the minds of both the minister and laity of the Church.

"There had been for many years a course of study laid out for those who wished to join the itineracy, on which they must pass examination before they entered. This had a wonderful effect to improve the minds of the ministers and to change their mode of preaching. There had been excellent literary societies formed in the Conferences, whose influences extended into the churches. These aroused, enlightened and refined the young people. Missionary societies had met with considerable success. They had a tendency to enlarge the hearts of Christians to assist their fellow-beings in the right way. The Sabbath-school work had taken a high stand. Sabbath-school Institutes were being held annually, which brought delegates from all parts of the State. These all gave most excellent reports of their proceedings.

"I was returned to St. John Chapel. All seemed satisfied with the appointment. After making arrangements for the winter, we entered into a protracted meeting. The week of prayer and preparation was largely attended, and the people seemed devoutly in earnest in seeking more of the presence of God. There followed a great outpouring of the Holy Spirit. There were many who professed religion and united with the church.

"After the revival meetings were over, we had time to look after other matters pertaining to the work of the church. I had been for some years district book steward and treasurer of the missionary fund, and also on the committee appointed to publish the minutes of the Conference. These things required considerable attention at times and added to my already heavy labors.

"The church membership was now so large that it was as much as one man could do to perform the duties incumbent upon him. The congregation and membership began to desire a new house to worship in. The old one had become too small to accommodate the large and intelligent audiences that were accustomed to meet there. The ground on which the old house stood was too narrow for the site of a larger church, so they began to look around for a more commodious location on which to build. We laid the matter before the church and the members freely acquiesced in the undertaking.

"The members and officers promised to do their best to raise money to begin with. The women entered freely into the spirit of the times. They held entertainments, and thus obtained considerable money, while they subscribed considerable amounts, which they paid in due time. They solicited the public and obtained their help. The men likewise did nobly to gather the necessary means.

"In the mean while we found a lot on the corner of Spruce and Cedar streets, in a very prominent part of the city, for which the owner proffered to take $5,000. But he finally agreed to let us have it for $3,200, which sum we agreed to give.

"The year of 1874 was drawing to a close and we began to make preparations for the Annual Conference which was to meet in Chattanooga, Tennessee, September 23, 1874. There was a large attendance at this Conference. The various stations and circuits brought in good reports. There had been refreshing revivals in most of them, and the outlook for the future of the Church was still hopeful. Many of the most faithful members had gone to join the innumerable host and Church of the first born, who stand in the presence of their glorified Redeemer forever.

"My report for 1874, was as follows: Members, 621; preachers, 6; Sabbath-school scholars, 600; teachers, 32; superintendents, 2.

"Though for a few years the epidemics had deccimated its members by many hundreds, yet the Church was still widening its influence and extending its borders, carrying progress and reform wherever it went. This was the first year we had served under presiding elders. Conference being ended, the ministers returned to their respective duties.

"I was appointed to St. John for the third time. As soon as I took charge I commenced to collect the money to pay for the lot on which to build. All the working members responded cheerfully. There was some delay necessary to ascertain all the facts, but a conclusion was finally reached, and we succeeded in paying the sum of sixteen hundred dollars ($1,600) through the course of the latter part of the year.

"The missionary question had received much attention that year. The ladies of the church had formed a mite missionary society, which collected and sent into the parent society the sum of one hundred dollars. The church held a large Sabbath-school convention in June of 1874, at which the majority of the ministers of the Conference were present.

"The old church needed some repairing which was done and all the expenses of the church were promptly met, and peace and harmony prevailed.

"The third year at St. John Chapel came to a close with many demonstrations of the affectionate regard that the people entertained for me. I prepared to remove to another field of labor. There had in my pastorate been more than five hundred members added to the church. Many infants had been baptized and many couples married. The sick and dying had always been attended to, and I had preached many funeral sermons. The Sabbath-school had more than doubled itself. Thus ended my third year at St. John Chapel.

"The Annual Conference was held in Avery Chapel, Memphis, Tenn., October 14, 1875, Bishop John M. Brown, presiding. The Conference was largely attended. How had the church increased in eight short years and extended its borders! When I commenced my labors in Tennessee, we had only one or two stations, a few small missions, and twenty ministers in all, who were members of Conference. Now in 1875, there were 98 preachers present. There were reported 10,189 members, 568 Sabbath-school teachers, 150 superintendents, and 8,234 Sabbath-school scholars. The retrospect to the work of those pioneer ministers was cheering indeed. They had borne the burden and heat of the day so long, and now as they descended the hill of life, the prospect was glorious indeed. In my report I gave in 872 members enrolled; 665 Sabbath-school scholars, and 89 probationers."

CHAPTER XIV.

"At the close of the Conference I was assigned to Payne Chapel, Edgefield, Tenn. I took immediate charge, called the members together, and preached my introductory sermon. The church was small and out of repair, the congregation was scattered. The few members that could be found seemed to be discouraged and inactive.

"I called the officers around me and laid the matters of the church before them. After making arrangements for my support, I began to visit the members and invited them to the church. They began to gather in from all sides and soon filled it. The classes were arranged and given proper leaders. Regular prayer-meetings were commenced and the members attended with great earnestness. We then began to make preparations for the winter by purchasing new stoves, and laying in fuel, and putting in gas fixtures. We then commenced our protracted meetings. The people assembled first for prayer and conference, and became so earnest that they invited their neighbors to join with them. Many soon began to show much concern for their salvation. Old men and young men, women and children, flocked to the anxious seat, and there began to be a wonderful outpouring of the Holy Spirit. Many hardened sinners were seized with conviction, and in a short time they were soundly converted to God.

"There were received into the church more than eighty men, some of whom related the most remarkable experiences, and commenced at once to live new lives. Great was the rejoicing when in the presence of one thousand persons they were immersed beneath the waves of the Cumberland river. The membership and congregation had grown too large to be accommodated in the church. It was generally filled by the Sabbath-school. So we proposed the expediency of putting an addition to the house and thus having it enlarged.

"The time was approaching that we should attend the General Conference, which was to meet in Atlanta, Ga., May, 1876, to which I had been elected a delegate the previous fall by the Tennessee Annual Conference. At the time appointed the ministers all convened and answered to the roll call. It was a pleasant and profitable session, but there were no Bishops elected that year. The matters of the Book Concern and the missionary question absorbed much of their time.

"After having adjusted all the other affairs of the church they adjourned, and the delegates all returned to their respective fields of labor. As soon as I returned I commenced to make preparations for repairing our church. The members rallied very willingly and gave money and other assistance, and there was soon an addition put to the house, which made it sufficiently large to hold the congregation. We painted the house outside and inside, and ornamented the pulpit and altar. This being done, we began to think of forming a choir. We obtained a teacher and formed a singing class, and purchased an organ, and when they were sufficiently drilled we built a choir gallery, and the choir took their seats. Our worship was both interesting and entertaining. The young people from all parts of the town came readily to assist in the worship. The Sabbath-school grew in size and interest daily, and many were the children who were gathered from the lanes and streets to learn the word of God. The influence of such an awakening could not help being felt in the surrounding community. The neighboring churches seemed to catch the spirit, and were revived in an unusual manner, and vied with each other who should do the most to advance the Redeemer's kingdom. Thus ended my first year in peace and prosperity.

"September 21, 1876, Tennessee Annual Conference was held in Pulaski, and thither at the appointed time the ministers assembled. Bishop A. W. Wayman, was the presiding officer. The business of the Conference was transacted with the usual alacrity, almost all departments of church work being in a prosperous condition.

"My report for that year was: Members, 159; Sabbath-school scholars, 170; teachers, 15; superintendents, 2. There had been some missionary work done, and our financial condition was good according to our number.

"At this period in the history of the Church the membership in the individual churches had been seriously affected by the restlessness of the people. They were compelled to make frequent removals in order to improve their condition. They often drifted from one part of the country to another to find employment; others purchased property and removed their membership when taking possession of their own homes in other districts. Again, many removed West, and their membership was taken away. Thus with all the usual number of members taken in the churches for a while, in some parts they could not much more than hold their own. But this difficulty was overcome in course of time by the people acquiring settled homes in great numbers, and confining their membership to those localities. But the reports of this Conference were good, considering the many difficulties through which they had to pass, for it was manifest that God was with them and had been their strength and support.

"At the close of the Conference I was returned to Edgefield Station, to the complete satisfaction of the people. I took immediate charge and began to make arrangements for another year's work. Hitherto they had not been able to give sufficient salary to support a minister and his family, but the membership still increased as I continued my pastoral visits and my exhortations to the people. The congregation still enlarged in size, and altogether they gave freely of their means, and thus afforded ample support so that the pastor was freed from secular care, and could devote all of his time to the work of the church.

"In the beginning of the winter of 1877, we commenced to hold protracted meetings. The church came together with one accord for supplication and prayer, and there was a glorious outpouring of the Holy Spirit. Many hardened sinners were drawn from the haunts of vice and iniquity, made a good profession before many witnesses, and were baptized into the church. There were many other precious souls added to the number, both youths and adults, all rejoicing in the consciousness of knowing that their sins were forgiven. Some of these converts, who were saved as brands from the burning, served as officers in the church and continue until to-day as pillars in the house of God. The Sabbath-school still grew in interest, and its influence among the young people was discernible on all sides. Some of our devoted members had gone up to join the Church of the first born, leaving a lasting testimony behind them, that the grace of God can save to the uttermost all who put their trust in him. Our people seemed to be advancing for the most part in all departments of society. Many were engaged in lucrative business, and their condition was becoming better daily. Many of the young men and women were attending the different colleges, and thus preparing themselves for future usefulness and light, and knowledge seemed to be diffused everywhere.

"The year of 1877 was now drawing to a close and we began to wind up our financial reports and other business of the year for the Annual Conference which was to meet in St. Paul Chapel, Nashville, Tenn., September 26, 1877. Although the Tennessee Conference had been divided previous to this time into Tennessee and West Tennessee Conferences, the attendance was large, there being sixty-six ministers present, beside many visitors. The Conference from the beginning was impressive and interesting. The missionary question received much attention and the collection was creditable. The Sabbath-school received more than usual attention by giving good reports, and many suggestions concerning its future advancement, winding up by celebrating a grand anniversary, which was participated in by all the Sabbath-schools of the A. M. E. churches of the city, and addressed by J. W. Early, B. Green, C. L. Bradwell, and others.

"I reported as follows: Members, 170; Sabbath-school scholars, 283; teachers, 18; superintendents, 1. Whole number of members belonging to the Conference, 6,611; traveling preachers, 52. The Conference showed a rapid increase since its division. I had for many years been Conference book steward, and had fulfilled all the duties of the office to the best of my ability. The auditing committee says this year, that they have found no discrepancy whatever in my accounts. The Conference closed in peace and harmony, and all the ministers returned to their labors much refreshed by their having assembled together."

CHAPTER XV.

"I was sent to Payne Chapel for the third time and began my labors with renewed vigor. This was a very pleasant and busy year. We held our protracted meetings in the beginning of the year 1878, and many were added to the church. Our classes were increased in number and had good leaders. The regular monthly communion was always well attended, and there seemed to be no falling off of membership; but a constant increase. Our force of local preachers was strong and active, and did some missionary work in the adjoining settlements and villages. Some of our number left us and went up to enjoy the rest prepared for the people of God. There was some repairing to be done and, the members cheerfully acquiescing, the work was soon accomplished.

"The year 1878 was now drawing to a close and we prepared to attend the eleventh Annual Conference of Tennessee, which was to meet in St. Paul Chapel, Fayetteville, September 26, 1878. We all assembled at the appointed time in the above place, Bishop Wayman, presiding. G. H. Shaffer was elected secretary. The number of members of the Conference was sixty-two. This was a more than usually interesting Conference, on account of the interest taken in the educational question. The efforts that had been made by the colored people to obtain an education, especially by African Methodists, were highly spoken of, and the institutions of learning which had been sustained by them received the highest commendation. A deep interest was shown in the missionary work. Both home and foreign missions were commended, and the collection for that purpose was good. The Bishop impressed upon the members of Conference the necessity of taking the *Christian Recorder,* the adopted paper of the Church, and expressed his hearty sympathy for the traveling ministers in their toils and hardships.

"The temperance subject received due attention, and the ministers were exhorted to preach on that particular subject once a year at least. The condition of the book concern was taken up and discussed and the ministers promised to do all in their power to assist it in its hour of deepest necessity. The reports all came in in due time and showed a great degree of prosperity on the part of the Church and ministry. I gave in my report as follows: Members, 242; local preachers, 6; Sabbath-school scholars, 332; teachers, 18; superintendents, 2.

"Having wound up the business of the church, I repaired to the Annual Conference, which met in Woodfork Chapel, Shelbyville, Tenn., October 15, 1879. Bishop A. W. Wayman was the presiding officer. The attendance was large and the proceedings heavy and interesting. The time had come to elect delegates to the General Conference which was appointed to meet in St. Louis, May 25, 1880. The election took place in due form and I received the highest number of votes, so that my name was first on the list of delegates. I was still treasurer of the missionary society; so it became my duty to receive the money that should be collected to defray the expenses of the delegates to the General Conference. The usual committees reported in good order: State of the Church, Temperance, Missionary, State of the Country. All departments were declared to be in a hopeful condition.

"This was my fourth and last year that I had served at Payne Chapel, Edgefield. I had the church repaired and painted and dedicated; had hung a small bell, and adorned anew the pulpit and altar. The members expressed their exceeding satisfaction with my efforts among them by numerous tokens of good will. While there I received into the church about four hundred and thirty members. Eighty men were added in one revival. They had sent in strong petitions each year for my return; but my time was out and I was necessitated to repair to another field. I gave in my report, which was as follows: Members, 247; local preachers and exhorters, 8; Sabbath-school scholars, 325; teachers, 18; superintendents, 2. Thus wound up a pleasant and profitable time at Edgefield, Tenn.

"When the appointments were read, I was assigned to Bethel A. M. E. Church, Nashville, Tenn. I took immediate charge after my return from Conference, but found the church overwhelmed with debt, and the house, which had been recently built, in the court for sale. They had erected a brick house and had paid nothing scarcely for the work and material. There was not a cent in the treasury. I went to the creditor and talked with him. He promised if we would pay him a certain amount he would desist from prosecuting the suit. I went to the judge of the court and talked with him, and by paying one hundred dollars cash, of my own money, we received the church free from the law. The house was without doors or lights or sashes in the windows, no plastering on the wall, and no seats. There were no stoves in which to make fires, and no means to get fuel. The winter was coming on with unusually stormy weather, and things looked gloomy indeed. We moved immediately into a little old dilapidated house which they had first used for a church, obtained some pieces of stove pipe and fixed up some old stoves, and commenced to hold meetings. The people who had been much scattered gathered in slowly.

"After committing our cause to God, we proposed to commence work. I laid my plans before them and some few agreed to help. The majority were discouraged, for they could see no way by which they could obtain sufficient money to pay for the bare necessities of the winter. We went to work and repaired the old house so as to make it endurable for the winter, and then I went around and invited my friends to come and assist us in our worship and entertainments. The members of the sister churches also lent us their aid, and encouraged us in our arduous undertakings. The young men and women from the Baptist College came over each Sabbath and helped with the Sabbath-school, which increased and became more interesting every week. We held several entertainments, from which we realized considerable sums with which to commence our work. Our first object was to plaster the house. We engaged workmen to do the job. The members began to come together and contribute as much as they could spare for the object. The public gave some and patronized our entertainments, so that the work went speedily on and bid fair to become a success. The plastering being done, we purchased doors and had them hung, paying for all as we went along. The windows we soon supplied with sashes and lights. We then purchased new stoves and had them put in. I went to the city authorities and asked them to have gas pipes run from the main on Division street, which was more than one square distant. They granted my request. We put in gas fixtures and had the house lighted with gas. I then went to the officers of a white Baptist Church, whom I knew to have surplus seats, and they readily let me have them, with which we seated the house. By this time the congregation had become of considerable size, the most of whom entering willingly into the work. We then bought an organ and loaned it to the church, and formed a choir.

"We had a pulpit erected, built an altar, and then invited the people to enter the church. Great was the joy when the people took possession of their almost finished house. The organ sounded, the choir sang, and the people shouted the praise of God, who had so signally assisted them in their work."

CHAPTER XVI.

"The month of May, 1880, having arrived we repaired to St. Louis, Missouri, to attend the General Conference, which was to meet there that year. This General Conference was full of interest from the beginning to the end. There were more than two hundred delegates present, and many fraternal delegates from various religious bodies. The delegates from the British Methodist Church from England visited the Conference and spoke encouragingly. There were three Bishops elected at that Conference, Rev. H. M. Turnner, Rev. W. F. Dickerson and Rev. R. H. Cain, who were ordained and initiated into office. There were many heated discussions on various topics by a number of young men who seemed to be present at such debates for the first time. There was also much enjoyment among the older and more experienced members when they took a retrospect of the progress of the church during the previous thirty years. How it had grown in numbers, in intelligence, in wealth and respectability and power! They also looked back at the great struggles it had passed through, and the poverty and persecution it had suffered--and now the Lord had brought them into a large place. They could but with exclamations and tears of joy give thanks to God for his unspeakable mercies to us as a people. The seasons of public worship were very interesting. The preaching was sublime, and showed a degree of thought and preparation not discernible heretofore.

"After the adjournment of General Conference I returned to my work much refreshed by my rest from such arduous toil. We commenced afresh to prosecute the work of building up the membership of the church. The students of the different colleges came to us and freely assisted us in our Sabbath-school, and the young people of the different churches helped us in our choir. They often came in numbers to aid us financially, and expressed their hearty sympathy for us in our great struggle, and thus God raised us up friends from every quarter. We called what few members there were together and consulted them on the propriety of holding a protracted meeting. They willingly assented to the proposition and commenced immediately to hold prayer meetings and preaching services. The praying members of the churches I had served heretofore came kindly to our assistance, and the ministers lent us their aid. There followed a deep concern among the people and there were a few conversions, which were added to the church.

"About this time many of the people removed to Kansas, and a number of my flock were among them, and this circumstance greatly diminished our numbers; but friends came again to our rescue, as they always had done when we were battling against great difficulties, and we were able by God's grace to triumph over every opposing force, and shout, "Victory!"

"We paid on the standing debt a considerable sum, and thus wound up our business for the first year at Bethel, in peace and comparative prosperity, to meet the Annual Conference in St. Paul Chapel, Columbia, Tenn., September 22, 1880, which was to be presided over by Bishop J. P. Campbell.

"The usual business of the Conference was enacted in due form. The members were all present, except one who had crossed over and gone to his reward. The various institutions of the church were reported in a prosperous condition. My report was as follows: Members, 116; exhorters, 2; Sabbath-school scholars, 131; teachers, 8; superintendents, 2.

"At the close of the Conference I was reappointed to Bethel Chapel, to the apparent satisfaction of all concerned, and immediately resumed my arduous toil. The year's labor was attended with the usual trials and triumphs which always attend the ministry in such charges. The ensuing winter was an extremely cold one, and the poor of the city suffered extremely for want of the necessities of life, which trials some of our little flock were bound to experience. But God who is always merciful, led us safely through the winter, and fair spring dawned upon us with its glorious sunlight and refreshing showers. We had quite a revival season and a number were converted and joined the church, and the membership more than doubled itself. The Sabbath-school increased and became more interesting. We had fine class meetings on one evening each week. Our preaching services were well attended on Sabbath, and we began to hope for a brighter future. We paid besides the current expenses of that year, the sum of $209.36. We were enabled to do much necessary work around the church: leveling the ground, clearing away rubbish, removing the old church, and fencing the new one to protect it from injury by rude persons who were always lurking around. Thus the second year of my pastorate drew to a close, and we began to prepare for the Annual Conference, to be presided over by Bishop J. P. Campbell, which was to meet in Payne Chapel, East Nashville.

"The attendance of Conference was very large, sixty-six members being present, besides many visiting brethren, who took an active part in the deliberations of the Conference. The ladies of the Conference formed a Mite Missionary Society, which realized a considerable sum of money which was sent to the treasurer of the Parent Missionary Society.

"The Conference also organized a literary society, designed to advance the intelligence of the ministry who had not enjoyed the advantages of theological training and other literary institutions. Many were the topics discussed relative to the extension of the Church, and the future success of its various institutions.

"The Committee on Temperance brought in some strong resolutions on the question, deploring the fact that some even of the ministry should indulge in that most degrading habit of social drinking."

This Conference, as did all others, paid due attention to the subject of Education, and always showed their zeal by the amount they contributed for that purpose. They appropriated every year some portion of their educational moneys for the benefit of Wilberforce University, as being the connectional school, and therefore all were under obligations for its support.

"The A. M. E. Church, notwithstanding the membership, was very much affected by constant removals. The number of members of the Tennessee Conference now stood at 7,663; total members of Sabbath-schools, 6,193. My report for the year was: Members, 134; Sabbath-school scholars, 197; teachers, 8; superintendents, 2.

"The Conference was continued from the 19th, to the 26th of October, 1881. Much against my will I was appointed by the Bishop to the presiding eldership of the first episcopal district, which included five counties, having 19 circuits and stations, with 37 appointments.

"After the adjournment of Conference, before taking charge of my appointment, I made a visit to St. Louis, my old and beloved home, and spent some days in company with those who remained of my former friends. There I reviewed with tearful interest the ground of my former struggles and labors. I then reviewed all my life, from my conviction and conversion and my long preparation to enter the active ministry; my abundant labors in introducing the work in many places, then seemingly barren, but now so fruitful of good results. I looked at our magnificent church, the result of pioneer labor, all along from the little cabin, up to a magnificent edifice which would do credit to any congregation. Then I asked for my colaborers: those who with me had encountered dangers untold, and had endured the storms of persecution so long. The manacles of slavery had long been unclasped from our limbs, and some of the most zealous in the work had gone on to join the number of the blessed before their eyes could see it; but now I had no doubt but that they were sensible of our improved condition and, rejoicing, gave honor and thanksgiving and blessing and glory to him who sitteth upon the throne, and to the Lamb who hath washed us in his own blood and made us kings and priests unto God.

"I visited the graves of my comrades, and there made a vow to take up the Cross anew, and buckle on the armor of the Gospel afresh, and march in the foremost ranks against the power of sin.

"Being much refreshed, I returned and took charge of my district and began to pursue my labors. I commenced at Edgefield Junction and went around the work, including Nashville, Knoxville, Chattanooga, Carthage, and all intervening places, encouraging the ministers, holding quarterly conferences, administering the Lord's Supper, visiting Sabbath-schools, helping to form new missions, making arrangements for suitable men to take charge of them, holding district conferences, at which we had very fine literary entertainments that seemed to attract the attention of many people, and large numbers gathered in to hear the efforts of the young ministers, and seemed well pleased at the results. We planned and built several new churches in the district that year, and the work went on both harmoniously and prosperously."

CHAPTER XVII.

"In traveling through the country where there were no railroads, we often encountered great dangers. At one time in order to reach Rome, Tenn., I was obliged to cross the Tennessee river in a canoe. The river, which is very broad, was overflowing its banks, and the boat was in a bad condition, being old and unsafe. When the word, "Ready" was given, I stepped in, but to my dismay six other men as heavy as myself came in also. When in mid-river the boat commenced to dip water and threatened to sink if we made the least motion. All were badly frightened. I knew that I could not swim a particle, and so I fled to God for refuge. I prayed earnestly that he would bring us safely to land and not permit us to go down in the deep and murky waters. The boat barely reached land, and I stepped out praising God for this signal deliverance.

"At another time I was compelled to go to an appointment on horseback. The animal afforded for that purpose was very old and clumsy. I mounted it and started, but in a short time after commencing my journey, the beast stumbled so violently that it threw me off over its head. I was stunned for awhile and badly hurt, but I soon was able to mount again and continue my journey, and reached my destination rejoicing in God and giving him thanks for his protecting power.

"Thus I labored through the district with all the energy of my being, until the close of the year, October 18, 1882, when the Annual Conference met in Chattanooga, Tenn. We came together full of hope and courage. The Conference opened, and was presided over by Bishop J. P. Campbell, assisted by Bishop R. H. Cain and Bishop J. A. Shorter. The visiting brethren were Rev. J. M. Townsend, Corresponding Secretary of Parent Home and Foreign Missionary Society; Rev. B. W. Arnett, Financial Secretary; and D. S. Bently, of the Kentucky Conference. The attendance of ministers was large, being 47 traveling and 12 local preachers, who were members of the Conference. The committees were active and intelligent, and gave good reports.

"On Sabbath-schools, the committee says in its report: 'We are glad to represent that the Sunday-school within the bounds of the Tennessee Conference is prospering as never before. The work is growing in numbers, in interest and efficiency; and yet there is room for more growth and larger additions to our numbers.'

"Of Education, the committee says: 'Education is the most popular demand of the day. We are living in a progressive age, and therefore the demand of the Church and school is becoming greater and greater from year to year. We, therefore, heartily endorse the course of studies prescribed in our Discipline by the last General Conference, and recommend the committees to be more careful in their examinations of candidates for the ministry.'

"The Temperance question, and also the Missionary cause, received much attention.

"The report of my district stands as follows: Membership, 2,567 (increase 472); probationers, 192; local preachers, 34; exhorters, 13; churches, 33; Sunday-schools, 38; officers, 72; teachers, 115; pupils, 1,776.

"The Ladies' Mite Missionary Society of Conference reported $50, which was promptly sent to the Parent Society, at Philadelphia.

"The business of the Conference having come to a close, our appointments were given us. I was stationed at St. John Chapel, Nashville, Tenn., in answer to a request from the officers.

"I received my appointment with reluctance, because for some time the church had not advanced, either financially or spiritually. The congregation was too small to afford means to defray the current expenses of the church, and the minister and people were not on the best of terms, and so the work of the church had entirely ceased. The foundation of the new church had been laid for more than three years, and no further work had been done on it. The old church was exceedingly out of repair. There was a large debt hanging over the membership, which they were making no effort to pay, and they were scattered and seemed to be discouraged. From the former experience I had I knew that it would be no easy matter to make a successful beginning under the existing circumstances.

"After bringing the matter before God, and asking his guidance and assistance, I made it my first object to hunt up the people and, if possible, bring them together. For this purpose I made many visits and talked with the members and endeavored to arouse them to see the necessity of repairing the old church; for it was not even in a condition to meet together in, let alone to worship God. It was hard to get the consent of the officers to attempt to do anything. The ladies were the first to come together, and to prepare for holding an entertainment to realize means with which to fix up the church. The brethren came in slowly, and the work commenced to move forward. The weather was cold and wet, and the windows were out, so that the wind blew in and the rain beat on the people when they met to worship. There were no fastenings to the doors. They stood open daily and any intruder could enter that chose. The seats were not fastened down to the floor, and some of them were broken, and the stoves were so worn out that there could be no fire. We made money enough to put in the windows and put locks on the doors and fasten down and repair the seats. I had credit with the merchants of the city, and they would afford me any necessary article on time payments. Therefore, I had coal laid in for the winter and gas furnished. We also bought new stoves and had them put up and the house thoroughly cleaned. The people then began to come in goodly numbers and to engage heartily in the worship. We rearranged the classes and set the leaders to work. This being done, by God's help, we commenced to hold a protracted meeting, which lasted some time. Many friends from the neighboring churches came in and assisted us in our exercises. There was much fervent prayer offered to God, asking him to meet with us. A season of refreshing from the presence of the Lord followed, and many professed conversion, who were taken into church and baptized, and assigned to their proper classes. We were enabled to meet the current expenses of the church so as to keep out of debt, and to hold our regular meetings. But the cloud still hung over us to some extent. It had gathered so densely and had been gathering so long, that it was no easy matter to dispel it. There were various causes at work, which we had no power to counteract, and we had no other resource but to trust God and do our duty."

CHAPTER XVIII.

"The ladies had formed a Church Aid Society, and had collected about six hundred dollars that year, hoping that in the course of two or three years to realize enough to commence building their new church. The Sabbath-school began to prosper, and many young people gathered together on Sabbath to worship God. The classes were well attended, and regular prayer meetings were kept up. We had the church painted inside and out, new carpets put on the floor, the pulpit decorated, and all things put in readiness for the close of the year. We paid all current expenses, the presiding elder's salary, and attended to other matters that were necessary for the benefit of the church, and then repaired to Conference, which was held at Franklin, Tenn., October 17 to 23, 1883, and presided over by Bishop J. P. Campbell, LL. D.

"There were at Conference about 74 preachers, members of the Conference, besides many visitors. There was considerable business to transact, among which was the election of delegates to the General Conference, which took place October 20, 1883. The contest was long and tedious, but finally ended with the election of the proper number, with their respective alternates. It was the first time since I had been an itinerate minister that I had not been elected a delegate to General Conference, but I felt quite resigned, for God in his inscrutable goodness had directed all my ways.

"The ladies of the Mite Missionary Society held a very fine meeting, which resulted in a good collection for the foreign missionary work, and was duly forwarded to the treasurer of the Parent Home and Foreign Missionary Society. The same officers were elected for the ensuing year.

"My report in the fall of 1883 stood: Members, 584; local preachers, 2; adults baptized, 35; infants baptized, 10; Sunday-school teachers, 17; pupils, 425. The total number of members reported to Tennessee Conference was 6,305. Our various interests belonging to the Church seemed generally in a prosperous condition.

"The Conference finished its business and we received our appointments. I was stationed at Salem Chapel, North Nashville, Tenn. This was

Page 133

the severest trial that I had ever experienced since I had entered the ministry. Surely my labors had been satisfactory the previous year and with the help of God I had brought the church into a prosperous condition, financially and spiritually, and the members all seemed to be in peace and harmony. These were the conditions I didn't find when I took charge in 1882. It was then that I became fully awake to comprehend the change that had taken place within a few years in the administration of the churches.

"The pioneer ministers had almost all passed away, with their zeal and uprightness, their godliness and capability. They had thrown aside all selfishness and had labored solely for the building up of the kingdom of Christ. The churches had advanced rapidly under their administration, and the membership lived in peace and tranquility, and the churches were kept in good repair, and the prospect always seemed bright for success in the future. But now another class of men had taken their places, in many instances, who showed but little earnestness or capability, although they had been blessed with better educational advantages. Yet the work did not prosper in their hands, and some of them always left the stations or circuits in a worse condition than they found them. I had found this to be the condition of the last four or five stations that I had taken charge of. It was no wonder, then, that I found myself reluctant to take up a work which I knew to be so completely run down. With much prayer and great earnestness I went and took charge. As usual from some mismanagement there were bickerings and divisions among the members, and they seemed to have lost confidence in themselves and every one else. And the work of the Lord seemed almost to have ceased. The church was sadly out of repair. Cold weather was rapidly coming on and there was no way to warm the house, for the stoves were worn out, and no money in the church treasury to buy new ones.

"I hunted up the officers of the church and tried to encourage them in their efforts to bring the members together. I visited all that I could find and invited them to come to the church. I went and bought stoves at my own charges and trusted to the members to pay me at their leisure. I then laid in fuel for the winter, prepared means for lighting the house better and had the seats all fixed, so as to better accommodate the congregation. In the meantime our regular services went on and the members began to be in better fellowship. During the latter part of the winter we commenced a protracted meeting at which there was a gracious outpouring of the Holy Spirit. Many were converted and added to the church and were zealous members ever afterward. I cannot forget many of those dear women who led off in bearing the expenses of the church, and in raising my support. Many times did they comfort me in their faithfulness to duty during my arduous labors among them, and I had reason to bless God often for such faithful companionship in the work of his holy cause.

"The month of May arrived, but I did not attend the General Conference which met in Baltimore, Md.; but staid at my work, trying to build up the spiritual interest of the church. The Sabbath-school claimed much of my attention. By exercising much labor and patience, I obtained many members to the Sabbath-school and it was in a prosperous condition. We had a regular prayer meeting established, and the classes flourished.

"The Conference year was thus drawing to a close, and in peace and prosperity the church prepared its financial matters for the Annual Conference, which was to meet in St. John Chapel, Nashville, Tenn., October, 1884.

"Nearly one hundred ministers were present at Conference, which was presided over by Bishop H. M. Turner, who was assisted by Bishop Wayman. It was a pleasant session. The services were sublime in the extreme. Bishop Turner in his own inimitable way conducted the ordination services, and the season was solemn and impressive to every one who was present.

"The Ladies Mite Missionary Society held a fine meeting, and there was contributed quite a sum to that cause. Meanwhile the committees were hard at work on the various topics before them, and finally gave in good reports. The resolutions were fine and well discussed. The visiting brethren seemed quite intelligent and took an active part, and all passed off smoothly and satisfactorily."

CHAPTER XIX.

"At the close of the Conference the Bishop, according to his best judgment, thought that I was needed at Columbia more than I was at Salem station, for Salem now was in a prosperous condition, and St. Paul, in Columbia, was out of order and run down. I accepted the charge and repaired to the field assigned to me. When I arrived, I found that there was much dissension and bickering among the members as to who should serve them. Some professed to favor one preacher, and some another. I paid no attention to the false representations which had preceded me, but took immediate charge and commenced the work.

"I called the officers together and laid my plans before them for the improvement of the condition of the church. It required some time to reassure the members and gather the classes together. I searched for the members in every part of the town and succeeded by the help of God in bringing them together. I turned my attention to the Sabbath-school. I hunted out the children and preached to them and tried to persuade the parents to send them in. In a short time many earnest youths were assembled to study the word of God.

"Peace and harmony now began to prevail among the members, and they became more regular in their attendance, and engaged heartily in the ordinances of the church. I found much to do before we could successfully move forward. The winter set in unusually severe. Money was hard to obtain, consequently there was some delay in fixing up the church and obtaining necessary fuel to keep good fires. The church had a number of stewardesses who were most excellent women and who did much to lighten the work of the pastor, and in keeping up the meetings. We established a regular prayer meeting, at which those who waited for the coming of the kingdom of Christ poured out their souls, invoking his presence and for a revival of his work.

"About the first of April, 1885, we held a week of prayer and preparation for a protracted effort. While doing so the people became throughly aroused and came together in large numbers. A revival and ingathering of souls followed, the like of which I had not witnessed for many years. The intensity and effectiveness of that religious awakening will never be forgotten by those who partook of its benefits until their latest hour. All the community, both old and young, seemed affected by it, and for some weeks nothing seemed to be thought of or talked about, but the great religious awakening and its results. Many of the most hardened sinners, who had defied the overtures of the Gospel for many years, yielded to its overwhelming power, and with tears of repentance acknowledged Christ as their Saviour. Drunkards and gamblers and Sabbath breakers alike bowed before the all-conquering power of God and owned Christ as a present Saviour. They were thoroughly converted and reformed from their old ways and became sober, industrious members of the church until the present day, standing still as the monuments of God's mercy in his own house.

"There was one incident which occurred in this revival worthy of particular notice. There was a certain young man who was a great scoffer, and who made it his business to ridicule those who made a profession of religion. One Sabbath morning during the revival he made some very unbecoming remarks to some persons who were about to start to church, and finished his tirade by saying, 'I believe that I will take my dogs up to the anxious seat the next time they call for mourners.' But just as he finished the sentence he dropped dead on the pavement. This, of course, created a great sensation.

"The ministers and members of the neighboring churches came in to assist in the work and beheld with wonder the manifestations of God's power. There were one hundred and fourteen souls converted and united with the church. The scene of so many being baptized in the river at one time was wonderfully interesting to all classes of persons, of whom a very great crowd was present. Great was the rejoicing among the old saints that their eyes should behold those for whom they had prayed so long become subject to the holy ordinances of the church.

"The names of all the candidates were enrolled on the class books and they were properly cared for each week. I found here how very useful were the faithful stewardesses in leading the young people's classes and their prayer meetings. Some of them made the most acceptable leaders that the church was served by, and now with joy unspeakable, and full of glory, we could exclaim, 'What hath the Lord wrought for us.' Peace and harmony and joy and good will prevailed everywhere, and everything moved on smoothly and prosperously in the house of the Lord.

"After the revival I was glad to take some rest, for my labors had been very severe. We adjusted our classes, renewed our officers, and attended to the other duties of the church. During the summer and early fall there had been some repairing done to the church and parsonage; but the year was drawing to a close and we began to prepare our financial report for the Annual Conference which was to meet in the month of October, 1885, in Pulaski, Tenn.

"Bishop H. M. Turner presided over the Conference. He was assisted by Bishop Disney of the British M. E. Church. The visiting brethren were: Rev. J. M. Townsend, Missionary Secretary, and Rev. B. W. Arnett, Financial Secretary of the A. M. E. Church. The business was conducted in a very lively and interesting manner. There was a very large attendance of ministers, and their reports were for the most part very encouraging. The committees transacted their business with faithfulness, and brought in many warm resolutions. The subjects of Missions and Education received more than usual attention. The Temperance reform was spoken favorably of, and the State of the Church highly commended, and while we looked with satisfaction over the past, we joyfully anticipated the future.

"The membership of the Church still increased as she widened her borders, and there was a constant accession of intelligent and active young people, who bid fair to be a blessing and help to our future progress as a people. When the reports of the members of the Conference were presented, mine was highly commended by both Bishop and Conference. The number of members was 380; Sabbath-school scholars, and teachers, 300. There was a petition read from St. Paul of Columbia for my return, which was granted by our Bishop. I was returned to the joy and satisfaction of all concerned. It was indeed very pleasant and satisfactory to myself to be reassigned to a place where my labors had been so successful, where I enjoyed the love and confidence of all classes of persons, both white and colored, and where I had received so many manifestations of their devotion."

CHAPTER XX.

"I took immediate charge on my return from Conference, and ordered my plans of work. We first gave the church a thorough repairing. We had it underpinned, the roof repaired, a fence built around it for its protection, and had it painted inside and out, and good flues built for the stoves. We went on prosperously until the latter part of the winter, when we concluded to hold a protracted meeting to see what the good Lord would do for us that year also. Our meetings had been well attended, peace and prosperity had reigned everywhere, and all enjoyed Christian fellowship and spiritual prosperity. We commenced our meeting by holding a week of prayer and preparation by fasting and meeting for mutual intercourse on the subject of religion and the preaching of the Word. The people came together in goodly numbers and joyfully entered into the work. Many persons showed a deep concern for the salvation of their souls. The meetings went on both night and day, and at all hours might be heard praise and prayer and thanksgiving to God for his unspeakable goodness to his believing children, and all seemed overwhelmed with the power of God. There were in the course of five weeks seventy-five hopeful conversions, all of whom joined the church, were baptized, and entered on the class roll.

"The same year the ladies of the church formed a society for the purpose of raising money to assist the officers in their efforts to make preparations to build a new church. Such was their energy and industry, that during the year they raised the sum of three hundred and thirty-nine dollars ($339) and laid it in the treasury, hoping soon to realize enough to commence building. During which time all the current expenses of the church were paid, the presiding elder's salary included.

"Thus the Lord blessed our labors the second year. We added during my pastorate more than two hundred members to the church, some uniting by letter, but the majority were new converts. My report was as follows: Members, 265; probationers, 12; local preachers, 14; Sabbath-school teachers, 19; superintendents, 2; scholars, 279. With this we repaired to the Annual Conference which was to meet in Chattanooga, Tenn., October, 1886, presided over by Bishop H. M. Turner, D. D., LL. D.

"The ministers came up to this Conference in goodly numbers, and with fair reports. Almost all the old fathers had passed away, leaving a memory sacred to all who knew them. They had encountered so many trials and surmounted so many difficulties while introducing the A. M. E. Church in the Southern States, and had led such upright and holy lives, that it was only with the deepest emotions that we recalled the memory of their presence among us. But now they rest from their labors and "their works do follow them." The ministers were few in number then, but now they had increased fourfold. Many new circuits had been laid out and many stations had been formed. Many houses of worship had been erected and thousands of members had been added to the Church. There had been also a great change wrought with regard to the salaries of the ministers within twenty years. When I first entered on the work in Tennessee, not one of the ministers received a liberal support. The best got but a small salary, many times not sufficient to defray their own expenses, let alone their families. But now all the stations gave a competency sufficient to meet all necessary expenses and to supply all their needs.

"Instead of persecution and abuse, we now receive general favor. No church is now held in greater esteem by the public than the A. M. E. Church. So much had been wrought through the mercies of God by their perseverance in good work and faithfulness to their duty and their godly examples in life and conversation. For intelligence and talent in the pulpit the ministers stand in the front ranks of God's ambassadors who proclaim the Gospel to men.

"The spiritual interest of the Church in general seemed good. The financial department made a fair report and the subject of education and missions had elicited considerable attention. It was an excellent proof of the advancement of our people, both religiously and socially, that they were willing to give so liberally of their hard-earned pittances for the establishment of the Gospel and the enlightenment of the race.

"The women everywhere stood in the foremost ranks in defraying the expenses of the Church. Although poor and overworked and weary, they always seemed to take delight in administering to the wants of the poor itinerant preacher, and of contributing to support his helpless family.

"At the close of the session when I received my appointment, it was to preside over the third district of the presiding elders,' which comprised five counties, with nineteen appointments with their circuits, including six stations. I bade farewell to the friends in Columbia whom I loved so dearly--

those with whom I had often enjoyed the most precious seasons of the outpouring of God's blessings, and who had shown to me such fervent love and unbounded confidence, and whom I shall always remember with the highest gratitude and the warmest affection, and began to make preparations to enter upon my new field of labor. I made out my appointments and sent them to the different ministers in the district, settled up my affairs and started. When I arrived I found that there was much to do and that the position was laborious and responsible.

"There were houses of worship needed in many places where there were considerable congregations who had no suitable place in which to worship. I commenced to try to stimulate the brethren to build in the various places where they were most needed.

"At Mooretown they went to work and erected a nice little edifice which they finished and dedicated 'St. James Chapel.' There perhaps is no class of people who do themselves more credit in building churches than the colored people of the South. According to their circumstances they give of their substance more cheerfully than those who own much more of this world's goods. There was a church erected at Calioca of sufficient size for the congregation, which they dedicated with much rejoicing. At Aspen Hill, there was a lively and wide awake congregation, who erected a church that would seat at least six hundred persons, which they finished and dedicated. There was a church built at Round-hill; also on Lynnville circuit, which was much to the edification of the membership who had labored faithfully to accomplish the work. At Hopewell, on Vale Mills circuit, there was built a good comfortable house of worship which added much to the interest of the A. M. E. Church in that place. At St. Matthews they built a nice little church, under the pastorate of Brother Lott Pegram. This was his last work on earth of church building. Not long after he was called to lay down his armor and take up the crown."

CHAPTER XXI.

"After passing around my district and holding the quarterly conferences in each circuit and station, we held our District Conference in Pulaski, where Elder W. J. Burch met us for the last time on earth. He seemed unusually solemn and thoughtful during the Conference, and expressed himself more than once that he felt there was some dreadful event before him which he would not be able to overcome. In a few days after he returned to his work. He left his two small children alone in the parsonage and, accompanied by his wife, went to the church to attend the funeral of one of his members. Just as they finished the interment there came a dreadful thunder storm. They took shelter together with seven others under a large tree. The lightning struck the tree and killed instantaneously all nine of the persons, besides their horses.

Thus the children were deprived of both parents at once, and the church of a beloved pastor, and the Conference of a faithful member. He went up, as we believe, from labor to reward.

The work of the year 1887 was now drawing to a close. We had held the electoral college and elected the lay delegates to attend the General Conference of 1888. They were elected and we began to make preparations to meet the Annual Conference, to be presided over by Bishop H. M. Turner, which was to meet at St. Paul Chapel, Nashville, Tenn., October, 1887.

"We gathered up our sheaves and repaired to the appointed place and were ready to answer to the roll call at the opening hour. There were more than one hundred ministers present, besides many visiting brethren. The Conference was full of interest from the beginning unto the end. The election of delegates was taken up at the proper time and the contest was unusually warm between the candidates. I was elected with a fair majority as a delegate to the General Conference to meet in the city of Indianapolis in May, 1888. The reports were good, and the Conference was an interesting and profitable one. The usual business was transacted with the accustomed interest, and all things passed off with the utmost good will and harmony. I was reappointed as presiding elder of the Third District. I took charge and spent the fall and winter in the arduous work attending my calling.

"The month of May arrived, and the delegates assembled in the city of Indianapolis, Ind., for the purpose of meeting in General Conference. When the roll was called, and I missed hearing the names of so many of those who formerly met in General Conference, a feeling of solemnity passed over me that I had never felt before. When so many who were younger than myself had ceased to labor, and had gone to inherit their reward, I felt sensible that this was the last General Conference I would ever attend as a delegate. I almost imagined that I could hear the voices of Revels, and Tyler, and Carter, and all those holy men who had done and suffered so much for the Church, calling me to finish the work assigned me, and prepare soon to enter my rest.

"After the opening of Conference, I was allowed some time to express my thoughts and desires, for there were many things which I wished to say to those who were now coming into the arena of action in the Church. The older members, with myself, felt that they were delivering to them a precious charge, whose cause would advance or retrograde according to the amount of zeal and energy they would afford to the work. There was much business transacted with reference to the future well-being of the Church, and I enjoyed much the interchange of affectionate conversation of my former friends. Many times did we thank God from the depths of our inmost hearts for his unspeakable goodness in permitting us to see the advancement of the Church we so faithfully labored to plant permanently in the world.

"There were four Bishops elected in the year 1888: Revs. B. W. Arnett, B. T. Tanner, W. J. Gaines and A. Grant. Toward the latter part of May, General Conference adjourned, and I returned to my labors with renewed vigor, passing from one point to another, endeavoring to encourage the brethren, holding quarterly conferences, administering the Lord's Supper, and striving to extend the work in all directions. In this year St. Paul, in Columbia, Tenn., was built, Willises Chapel erected, also the Bear Creek Mission established, Water Valley and Lilborn Missions extended, and many other things accomplished that had a tendency to forward the Gospel of the Lord Jesus Christ.

"The Sabbath-schools were looked after with intense interest. Teacher's institutes were held in different parts of the country, and representatives of Sabbath-schools often met to talk over plans for the future advancement of the Church in obtaining a proper knowledge of Bible truths.

"The cause of education was propagated, according to our best ability, and so the year passed full of good works crowned with many blessings, until its labors came to a close in October, 1888, when we were summoned to the Annual Conference which was to meet in Columbia, Tenn. It was presided over by Bishop A. W. Wayman, who was appointed by the committee of Bishops at our last General Conference to preside over our district.

"The number of ministers in attendance was very large, and the business of the Conference full and perplexing. There were many changes made that year--some to the detriment, and others to the well-being of the Church. I accepted no appointment from that year forward."

And thus ends the active labors of one who had been on the battle field for fifty-two years, exerting all his powers to do the will of Him that sent him. Great and marvelous were the changes that had taken place in those years. At the beginning of his work the spirit of slavery was exerting its strongest influence, and oppression and persecution were rife everywhere, and dangers and trials opposed them on every hand. Their numbers were small, and the name, "African Methodism," with many was only a hiss and a byword. "But, now," says he, "as my physical constitution gives way under the weight of many years of toil, and my mental powers begin to abate their ardor through long sieges of conflict with the fierce enemies of the Cross, and I begin to unharness my armor to lay it at the Master's feet, with the highest gratitude I can stand with congregated thousands of the blood-bought throng, and give honor and praise and thanksgiving and power to Him who giveth us the Victory through our Lord Jesus Christ. And, though a veteran soldier, I must take my discharge and watch the conflict while others fight in the sacred ranks, my heart still glows with zeal for the success of the beloved Church, whose cause I so early espoused, while I begin to make preparations to meet my beloved companions and colaborers who have preceded me to join the everlasting song of the Church of the first born."

CHAPTER XXII.

Early was always imbued with a spirit of reform, and engaged with heart and soul in promoting the great reforms of the day. He early in life enlisted in the antislavery cause, and though subject to the utmost vigilance of the slaveholding communities in which he lived, he always extended a helping hand to that unfortunate class of persons who were oppressed beyond the power of endurance by the existing system of slavery. Many times he with others, who were equally interested in the well-being of oppressed humanity, would make great and successful efforts in buying and emancipating men and women from slavery, who afterward made good and useful citizens.

He was a strong advocate of the temperance reform, often engaging in their meetings and speaking to the people on the important topics connected with the temperance question. He was always ready to visit the sick and destitute. Often when he was made acquainted with their wants and sufferings he would give to them his necessary spending money, and deny himself of many comforts on that account. So tenderly did he care for the sick and dying that perhaps he was called upon to preach a greater number of funeral sermons than any other minister in the Connection. He was called by special request to perform the burial rites for hundreds of his own members, besides many friends who were members of other churches.

He was a favorite with the young people in every community in which he labored. The students of the different colleges seemed to consider it their especial duty to assist him in his Sabbath-schools and all social gatherings of the church. They never seemed to forget to invite him to their entertainments.

His love for the A. M. E. Church was unbounded. He was always ready to defend the rights of his denomination and to cherish its smallest interests. He joyfully spent the best years of his life in trying to establish and build up the Church he so much loved, enduring every species of hardships and toil, and often suffering great deprivations that he might win many souls to Christ and enlarge the borders of the Church. He always entertained the highest appreciation for the obligations and duties incumbent upon his position as an ambassador for Christ, and strove to maintain an upright and godly character.

He served the Church in the capacity of Conference Book Steward for the space of twelve years, while a member of the Tennessee Conference. For quite a number of years he was treasurer of the Conference Missionary Society, and a part of the time Conference treasurer. He always served on one or more of the most important committees appointed by the Bishop at each Annual Conference. And while a member of the General Conference for more than thirty years, served on some of the most important committees attendant on that august body. Always faithful and vigilant, never for a single moment remiss in his duty. He was a great lover of the Sabbath-school cause and was president of the Sabbath School Union of the city of Nashville for some time, until he took a charge out of the city. He was from early life a member of the Masonic Fraternity, and in later life a member of the Knights of Wise Men, which membership he held with honor and fidelity.

He performed the marriage ceremonies for not only his own members, but for many others outside of the pales of the Church. He sometimes would unite more than a hundred couples during one pastorate. He was a strong advocate of education, exerting himself with all his power to give his children the best educational advantages to be had in their day. He was an earnest supporter of Wilberforce University, as being the adopted school of African Methodism. Besides sending his children and keeping them there for a number of years, he contributed largely of his money for its support, and was the means of inducing many students to attend the school.

He was particularly earnest in his solicitude for the prosperity of young ministers, always striving to encourage them to prepare for greater usefulness, and urging them to fulfill with acceptance the great duties of life which pressed upon them. When any one expressed a desire to come before the public or that he felt a call to preach the Gospel, Early had a peculiar art in the power to induce him to enter some field of usefulness, so as to acquire the necessary experience to encounter the difficulties of appearing before the world as an expounder of the Gospel. Thus many very useful men attribute their start in life to his influence. He always seemed happy when he could present a young man before his class for license to preach, or recommend him to his Conference for deacon's or elder's orders.

J. W. Early always seemed to enjoy the intercourse of friends with a hearty relish. He would spend much time in giving such advice as he was able, and imparting to others what he had learned from his experience in his ministerial and other labors. He was charitable to all benevolent purposes with which he was acquainted, and gave freely of his means to assist the poor. He was hospitable to strangers, and especially to the ministers of the Gospel. The wayfaring servant of God always found a welcome place by his fireside. In the early days of the Church, when its friends were few and its means small, he says, "A great part of my income was spent in entertaining the ministers and Bishops of the A. M. E. Church, even before I joined the itinerancy." He loved to detain them as long as possible near their work on account of the prosperity of the Church.

J. W. Early was married twice. In the year 1843, on the 6th day of June, he was married to Miss Louisa Carter, in the city of St. Louis, Mo. The ceremony was performed by Rev. Byrd Parker. The marriage was a happy one, and they were the parents of eight children, four of whom reached the years of maturity. Mrs. Early was an amiable Christian woman, and one who was highly esteemed by all who knew her. In the year 1862 she was called from earth to join those of her happy family who were gone before, leaving with her friends a sweet remembrance of her many virtues and good deeds done to the poor and needy.

J. W. Early remained unmarried nearly seven years, when on the 24th day of September, 1868, he again entered into the marriage relation with Miss Sarah J. Woodson, of Berlin, Ohio.

This lady entered fully into the work of the Gospel with him, assisting in all of his most arduous duties, and sharing most cheerfully with him all his hardships, deprivations, and toils. She always assisted in superintending the Sabbath-schools when near enough to reach them; always attending and often leading the prayer meetings; and she took an active part in visiting the sick and administering to the wants of the poor and needy, and in raising money to defray the expenses of the Church, and served most heartily in its most laborious duties, and engaged extensively in its educational work. Mrs. Early is best known to the public by being so widely employed in the temperance reform.

J. W. Early was always a bountiful provider for his family, always solicitious for their well-being, and careful to supply all of their wants.

He was an affectionate father, indulgent to his children, even in their mature years. His name will always be held in grateful remembrance by those who have shared his bounty and received his benefits

And thus ends the life work of one of God's most faithful servants, who is now only awaiting the call of his Master to ascend and unite with his comrades who have gone on before, and join with the thousands whom he received into the Church to praise the Eternal who sits on the throne, and to adore the Lamb.

"There all the ship's company meet,
Who sailed with their Saviour beneath;
With shouting, each other they greet,
And triumph over trouble and death."

HISTORIC PULISHING
2017

www.ingramcontent.com/pod-product-compliance
Lightning Source LLC
Chambersburg PA
CBHW050356100426
42739CB00015BB/3413